Reading and Interpreting
the Works of

CORMAC
McCARTHY

Lit Crit Guides

Reading and Interpreting the Works of

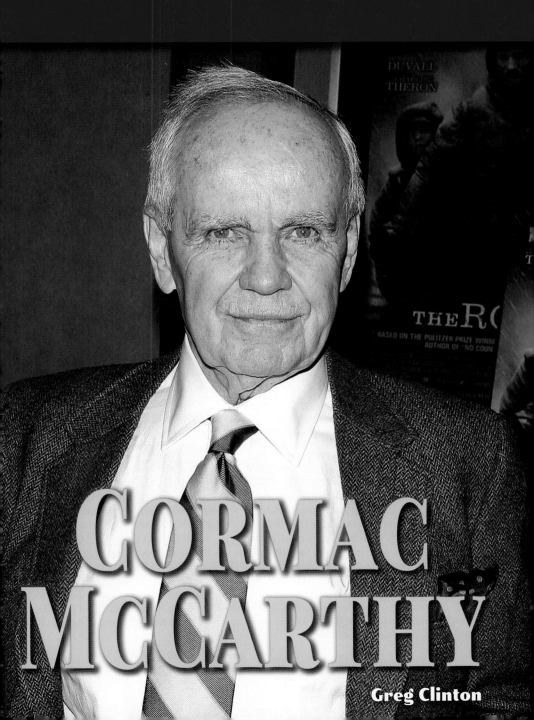

CORMAC McCARTHY

Greg Clinton

Published in 2017 by Enslow Publishing, LLC
101 W. 23rd Street, Suite 240, New York, NY 10011

Library of Congress Cataloging-in-Publication Data
Names: Clinton, Greg.
Title: Reading and interpreting the works of Cormac McCarthy / Greg Clinton.
Description: New York, NY : Enslow Publishing, 2017. | Series: Lit crit guides | Includes bibliographical references and index.
Identifiers: LCCN 2015048249 | ISBN 9780766079151 (library bound)
Subjects: LCSH: McCarthy, Cormac, 1933---Criticism and interpretation--Juvenile literature.
Classification: LCC PS3563.C337 Z597 2016 | DDC 813/.54--dc23
LC record available at http://lccn.loc.gov/2015048249

Printed in the United States of America

To Our Readers: We have done our best to make sure all website addresses in this book were active and appropriate when we went to press. However, the author and the publisher have no control over and assume no liability for the material available on those websites or on any websites they may link to. Any comments or suggestions can be sent by e-mail to customerservice@enslow.com.

Photo Credits: Cover, pp. 3, 87 Jim Spellman/WireImage/Getty Images; vectorgraphics/Shutterstock.com (series logo); p. 6 Andrew H. Walker/WireImage/Getty Images; p. 11 Columbia Pictures/Getty Images; p. 15 Macha/ullstein bild via Getty Images; p. 17 Robert Alexander/Getty Images; p. 20 Everett Historical/Shutterstock.com; p. 24 http://www.archive.org/details/ghostseero1schiuoft/Wikimedia Commons/Frankenstein.1831.inside-cover.jpg/public domain; p. 27 Everett Collection/SuperStock; p. 34 MPI/Archive Photos/Getty Images; pp. 36, 39 Herbert Orth/The LIFE Picture Collection/Getty Images; p. 48 Rolls Press/Popperfoto/Getty Images; pp. 52, 63, 66, 100 A.F. Archive/Alamy Stock Photos; p. 56 Sarah L. Voisin/The Washington Post/Getty Images; pp. 60, 80 DeAgostini/Getty Images; p. 70 Kean Collection/Archive Photos/Getty Images; p. 72 Victoria & Albert Museum, London, UK/Bridgeman Images; p. 78 Bildagentur Zoonar GmbH/Shutterstock.com; p. 85 Hulton Archive/Getty Images; p. 92 © Photos 12/Alamy Stock Photo; p. 94 Israel Hervas Bengochea/Shutterstock.com; p. 104 Topical Press Agency/Hulton Archive/Getty Images; p. 108 © ZUMA Press, Inc./Alamy Stock Photo.

CONTENTS

Cormac McCarthy

Introduction

An Unmistakable Author

One thing is for certain: You can't mistake a novel by Cormac McCarthy. The way he uses language is unique in contemporary fiction. Reading his stories can sometimes feel like you've been transported to another age, an ancient time when the planet was profoundly symbolic of some universal force. McCarthy uses words that no one else uses, or hasn't used in a hundred years, or are from languages other than English, words like *salitter*, *swale*, and *sotol*. Even if you don't know what these words mean (they are obscure references from seventeenth-century mysticism or North American ecology) they seem to resonate on the page. His writing sounds different. Along with his archaic vocabulary, McCarthy draws out his sentences into rambling journeys of their own, connecting clause upon clause with image after image. No one else in the literary world today has such a distinctive style. Cormac McCarthy is unmistakable.

The themes he explores are darkness, the lack of objective meaning in the world, the question of good and evil, and the inevitability of death. This is not literature for kids. In McCarthy's worlds, people and animals die horrifying and brutal deaths and are subjected to terrible torture and suffering. There is no "happily ever after." Human beings are only occasionally heroic, and even when they are, they don't often succeed in their quests.

McCarthy portrays a masculine world; women don't figure very prominently in any of his fiction. Men are *men*. They take things, they don't show fear or emotion, they ride, they conquer, they drink, and they kill. This is a point of criticism for some readers. Critic James Wood has called his masculinism "claustrophobically male-locked: McCarthy has a tendency to omit half the human race from serious scrutiny."[1] Other critics note that his focus is white males, rather than accounting for the perspective of other races.

Even if these assessments of McCarthy's body of work are true, it is still a remarkable collection of stories, almost unmatched in the past hundred years. What follows is an attempt to illuminate this difficult, strange, and beautiful collection of novels and stories. In a way, this is impossible. McCarthy's work is almost impossible to classify: Is *Blood Meridian* a Western? A parable? Or an allegory? McCarthy's fiction doesn't fit neatly into genres, as we will see in the following chapters. In order to make some sense of the works of McCarthy, this book will focus primarily on the second half of his career, on his major novels: *Blood Meridian*, The Border Trilogy (specifically *All the Pretty Horses* and *The Crossing*), and *The Road*. Some comparisons will be drawn to early novels as well as *No Country for Old Men*. The early novels are interesting for historical perspective, but the later novels are the works that display McCarthy's full talents and stylistic mastery.

allegory
A story that contains a hidden moral or meaning.

parable
A short story that teaches a lesson or illustrates a religious principle.

What you encounter in this book will never be a substitute for the original thing, just like an essay about a symphony will never substitute for hearing it firsthand. You must read the words themselves.

Steel yourself: McCarthy's work is not for the faint of heart. It requires courage.

A Slow and Steady Rise to Prominence

Cormac McCarthy doesn't like attention. He has granted only a handful of interviews in his career. He has only participated in a single television interview, with Oprah Winfrey in July 2007 after the publication of his Pulitzer Prize–winning novel *The Road*. Even when he was a critically acclaimed author in the 1960s through 1980s, he never used the strength of his work to get rich or famous. In 1985, when he published what many regard as his masterpiece, a novel called *Blood Meridian, or, The Evening Redness in the West*, it was not a massive critical or commercial success: The book sold fewer than 5,000 copies. In fact, none of his early books sold well, and he was not a household name by any measure. But in 1992, McCarthy published the first of his Border Trilogy, *All the Pretty Horses*. That novel won the National Book Award and the National Book Critics Circle Award, two extremely prestigious marks of serious literary achievement in American fiction. It was also a best seller, and in 2000 it inspired a mediocre but nonetheless star-studded Hollywood adaptation starring Matt Damon and Penélope Cruz, directed by Billy Bob Thornton.

Stardom Late in Life

Since the success of *All the Pretty Horses*, McCarthy's star has risen, and fast. He is routinely described as the greatest living American author. *Blood Meridian* is on *Time* magazine's list of the 100 greatest novels written in the English language, and on

Several of McCarthy's novels have been adapted for film, including *All the Pretty Horses* in 2000, starring Matt Damon and Penélope Cruz.

APPEARING ON TV: THE OPRAH INTERVIEW

Cormac McCarthy has only ever done one television interview, so this one is worth looking at for a few moments. The singular televised conversation was with Oprah Winfrey, taped at the Santa Fe Institute—McCarthy's home turf—in a reading room. McCarthy seems entirely uncomfortable with the process throughout the session. But he says a number of interesting things, and from this conversation we can glean insights into his way of thinking and writing.

The interview was recorded to mark the occasion of McCarthy's novel *The Road*. Oprah has styled herself a champion of literacy and her endorsement always drives massive sales among American readers. During the interview, McCarthy is slouched down in his leather chair, head resting on his chin almost as if he's ready to fall asleep. He answers Oprah's questions with gentle humor and thoughtfulness, even so. It might be the most accessible he's ever been in public, so any fan or interested reader should watch the clips from the interview, which are hosted on Oprah's website.[1]

McCarthy is not self-aggrandizing; he doesn't strike a pose and hope that people think he's a superhero writer.

"Are you passionate about writing?" asks Oprah. McCarthy pauses for a moment in thought. "I don't know," he replies. "Passionate sounds like a pretty fancy word. I like what I do. . . . You always have this image of the perfect thing which you can never achieve." He's striving after the perfect thing, the project that's in his mind, but he knows he'll never produce it perfectly.

Why doesn't McCarthy do interviews? (He's only ever done a handful in print, and this one on television.) "I don't think it's good for your head," he says simply. As a writer, he "probably shouldn't be talking about it," instead he should be "doing it." He isn't implying that television isn't important work. "You work your side of the street, and I'll work mine," he chuckles.

Does Cormac McCarthy believe in God? This is a complex question that his fans would want to know in greater detail—so much of his writing is infused with religious thought and language. "It depends on what day you ask me. Sometimes it's good to pray. I don't think you need to have a good idea who God is to pray," he says. This response lines up with his fiction, which presents the sacred without pinning it down to a particular tradition or dogma.

many top American literature lists. Influential literary critic Harold Bloom has championed McCarthy as a genius, a star to sit next to the likes of Herman Melville, William Faulkner, and Ernest Hemingway, and maybe to eclipse them.

Following *Blood Meridian*, the Border Trilogy yielded three extraordinary novels, but McCarthy was hardly finished (and as of this writing, at eighty-two, he is said to be hard at work on three more novels). In 2005 he published *No Country for Old Men*, which inspired the Coen brothers to adapt it into a film in 2007, which won four Academy Awards, including Best Picture. McCarthy published *The Road* in 2006 to enormous critical and commercial acclaim. That novel garnered the Pulitzer Prize for fiction, and perhaps more importantly for sales, a spot on Oprah Winfrey's book club. Oprah convinced him to do his one and only television interview. *The Road* was also adapted to the screen in 2009, and while it didn't win any Oscars, it is a faithful rendition and generally excellent film. In between novels McCarthy has had time for a handful of screenplays, all of which were adaptations of his own novels or plays for the big screen, except for the 2013 feature film that he wrote called *The Counselor*, directed by Hollywood legend Ridley Scott. It starred superstars Brad Pitt, Michael Fassbender, Cameron Diaz, Penélope Cruz, and Javier Bardem.

A Brief Biography

Born in Providence, Rhode Island, in 1933, Cormac (originally "Charles") McCarthy moved with his family to Knoxville, Tennessee, in 1937. His father was a well-educated and successful lawyer who valued education. After a year at the University of Tennessee from 1951 to 1952, Cormac joined the Air Force and was stationed for a couple of years in

McCarthy lived in El Paso, Texas, for almost twenty years. It was in this border city that he wrote several of his most acclaimed novels, all set in Texas and Mexico.

Alaska. He went back to the University of Tennessee in 1957 but never finished his degree, dropping out in 1961 to wander and finish work on his first novel, *The Orchard Keeper*, which won the William Faulkner Foundation Award for best debut novel by an American.

The places where McCarthy lived and worked had a deep influence on his choice of setting for his first novel. Growing up in Tennessee gave him the background and context to write *The Orchard Keeper*, set in the Appalachian hills, as well as *Outer Dark* in 1968 and *Child of God* in 1973, the story of a necrophiliac serial killer living in a cave in rural Tennessee. (This novel is based on real events.)

In 1976, McCarthy moved to El Paso, Texas, where he began studying the border country. After the 1979 release of *Suttree*, his attention seemed to fully shift to the southwest and to Mexico. In 1981 he was awarded a MacArthur Fellowship, which is often called the "genius grant." This gave him a financial cushion while he worked on what would be his great masterpiece, *Blood Meridian*, published in 1985. Reviewers took notice, even though the book didn't sell as well as it would later. It's been called a "cold-blooded masterpiece" and a "lean nightmare."[2] For many literary critics and academics, *Blood Meridian* is as important a book as Herman Melville's *Moby-Dick*.

For the next few years, McCarthy worked on what would be his Border Trilogy. *All the Pretty Horses* came out in 1992, winning him commercial and critical fame. *The Crossing*, the second and most complex novel in the trilogy, was published in 1994 and featured more landscape and setting from the El Paso and northern Mexico region. The final book, *Cities of the Plain*, out in 1998, was less complex and intense than the previous two, but rounded out the stories of John Grady

McCarthy's novels, which cross over into multiple genres, explore themes including morality, religion, and violence.

Cole (from *All the Pretty Horses*) and Billy Parham (in *The Crossing*), having them become friends and colleagues.

The final novels—*No Country for Old Men* and *The Road*—both stem from McCarthy's Southern roots. Interestingly, while *No Country* is still set in the Texas borderlands, *The Road* wanders to the east. McCarthy is reportedly working on a novel set in New Orleans, tentatively titled *The Passenger*. So, while his literature is rooted in his travels and where he lives, it is clear that his career is not routine, that he is always pushing at the edges of the map.

THE DARK WORLD OF McCARTHY'S FICTION

If you read enough of Cormac McCarthy's novels, you should begin to suspect that there are dark mysteries buried under the surface of his characteristic florid and stark prose. McCarthy is often compared with nineteenth-century German philosopher Friedrich Nietzsche, who famously exposes what he argues are the weaknesses of the Judeo-Christian worldview and diagnoses the dangers of a nihilistic (or, essentially meaningless) existence. For Nietzsche, the salvation of humanity isn't Christ, but creativity and art. In McCarthy's fiction, though, readers will find a great deal of the meaninglessness, the "void" as he likes to describe it, and very little of the salvation. To read McCarthy is often a project of coming to terms with death and violence without an explanation or a clear path to understanding. It can be a journey of despair. This is literature that gets going and won't let go—it never flinches from real human suffering, and it dwells in the darkest places.

Archaic Language

Every writer builds on the past, and the great authors do something original with their storytelling, whether by creating new and unusual characters, by changing the way they construct a narrative, or perhaps by addressing some topical or controversial theme. There is no one who

florid

Extremely complicated or elaborate.

Parallels are often drawn between McCarthy's stark writings and the nihilistic beliefs of German philosopher Friedrich Nietzsche.

sounds like Cormac McCarthy. His use of language is absolutely distinctive, with its mixture of poetic rhythm, arcane vocabulary, dazzling precision, and sweeping vision. The final words of one of his most famous novels, *All the Pretty Horses*, provide a sense for how he places a character—in this case, a cowboy riding a horse, leading a second horse—inside a landscape and then supercharges the description with extra meaning:

> The bloodred dust blew down out of the sun. He touched the horse with his heels and rode on. He rode with the sun coppering his face and the red wind blowing out of the west across the evening land and the small desert birds flew chittering among the dry bracken and horse and rider and horse passed on and their long shadows passed in tandem like the shadow of a single being. Passed and paled into the darkening land, the world to come.[1]

The dust is not just red, it is *bloodred*. The sun doesn't shine on his face, it is *coppering* it. Their shadows don't just mingle, they are *like the shadow of a single being*, and this simple metaphor speaks to the entire novel, to the relationship between this cowboy and the horses with which he works so expertly and lovingly. Even if a reader doesn't happen to know words like *bracken* or *chittering*, and even though *bloodred* is a manufactured word, we can read McCarthy's prose like it was poetry. Each word, each phrase, seems to have exact value and incredible intensity. Words aren't wasted.

Before we delve into the literature itself, it's important to pay attention to the styles, symbols,

metaphor

A figure of language identifying two things that are not similar in order to enhance the meaning or significance of something.

and themes that recur in McCarthy's work. It's also important to understand where his writing fits into the history of literature. Specifically, we should take a look at the idea of Southern Gothic writing, with which McCarthy is often associated, and also with the religious philosophy known as gnosticism.

What Is Southern Gothic?

The type of literature that has been called Southern Gothic is the intersection of two different traditions: stories from the American South, and an older Gothic genre that originated in Europe in the eighteenth and nineteenth centuries. Most people are probably familiar with stories like *Frankenstein* and *Dracula*. Mary Shelley's *Frankenstein* was a huge hit after it was published in 1818, and it remains enormously popular. Bram Stoker published *Dracula* in 1897, and vampires have never really gone out of style since then. These two stories are useful models for the Gothic tradition because they both feature dark, mysterious, "freakish" creatures, and readers are supposed to be thrilled by the grotesque violence they encounter in the texts.

Freaks in the Gothic Tradition

The attention that Gothic texts give to "freaks" is important, since Gothic horror stories became popular in response to an intellectual movement known as the Enlightenment. The Enlightenment was a time in early American and European history when people started to believe that they could use rationality and logic to shape a perfect society; that they could use the tools of science to know everything there was to know, and they could control the environment and use it for human purposes. In some ways, the Enlightenment was very powerful. It gave us modern forms of democracy, since people in France and the newly formed United States stopped trusting "divine" kings to rule them effectively. And the rise of science has had far-reaching effects on society: We have incredible technology for communicating and traveling, we have unlocked amazing knowledge about the stars and about atoms, we have used science to create new medicine and technologies of health that have expanded the average life span, and so on.

Despite all of its benefits, there was a reaction against the Enlightenment during that same period, a movement whose effects still linger in modern society, known as Romanticism. The Romantics wanted to keep the mysteries of the universe that the Enlightenment promised to uncover. They thought that Nature (with a capital "N") could never be dominated by humans. They believed that science was fine and good, but it would never allow humans to know *everything* there was to know; knowledge was essentially limited. And they revived a feeling of the sacred, or the older religious, supernatural feelings that the Enlightenment wanted to replace with logic and reason.

So when Gothic writers focused on freaks like Frankenstein's monster, or the eerie and magical vampire in Transylvania, they wanted to emphasize what was not normal, what did not conform to the uniform, rational image of "human" or "natural." They wanted to emphasize the mystery that remained in the world, even while science tried desperately to rationalize everything. Gothic literature, even when it falls under the category of science fiction, draws heavily from Romanticism.

America Goes Gothic

Something similar happened much later, in the nineteenth and twentieth centuries, in American Southern literature.

An illustration from an early edition of Mary Shelley's 1818 novel *Frankenstein*. Certain elements of Shelley's Gothic style can be found in McCarthy's work.

What became known as the Southern Gothic tradition is an extension of the European Gothic tradition, since the stories also focus on abnormal, freakish, weird, or violent characters and events. And in some ways, Southern Gothic stories could be thought of as a reaction to the North, which would win the American Civil War and proceed to impose a culture of reason and Enlightenment ideals on a Southern culture steeped in Afro-Caribbean folklore, racism, and violence.

Cormac McCarthy is often described as a Southern Gothic writer since his stories rely on the setting—the American South or Southwest (although his shift to the Southwest forced critics to think about his work differently, especially regarding the construction of racial differences and cultural markers)—as well as violent, unusual, dark, mysterious situations and events. For example, in his early novel *Outer Dark*, a young woman bears her brother's child, and after he leaves the infant to die in the woods, she sets out (in vain) to find him while her brother wanders in search of redemption (which he never finds). *Child of God*, another early novel, tells the story of a disturbed Tennessee man who devolves deeply into a violent, murderous life on the fringes of society and finally, off the grid entirely. *Blood Meridian*, perhaps McCarthy's masterpiece, is one of the bloodiest novels in American literature, a Western with no good guys and a decidedly unhappy and unsettling ending. McCarthy takes violence and darkness to another level of intensity, and this is prob-

---

redemption

The act of saving someone who is considered "lost."

---

ably one reason he has been set apart as a novelist from the rest of contemporary American fiction, and what has garnered him so much attention.

A useful question to ask might be: Why do McCarthy's works fit the Southern Gothic model, but also, how are they distinct? And this question will lead us to a related question: What is the purpose of violence in McCarthy's stories?

The Grotesque and Mystery

In an essay titled "Some Aspects of the Grotesque in Southern Literature," the great American author Flannery O'Connor writes:

> If the [Southern] writer believes that our life is and will remain essentially mysterious, if he looks upon us as beings existing in a created order to whose laws we freely respond, then what he sees on the surface will be of interest to him only as he can go through it into an experience of mystery itself. His kind of fiction will always be pushing its own limits outward toward the limits of mystery . . . Such a writer will be interested in what we don't understand rather than in what we do. He will be interested in possibility rather than in probability. He will be interested in characters who are forced out to meet evil and grace and who act on a trust beyond themselves–whether they know very clearly what it is they act upon or not.[2]

In other words, for O'Connor—whose stories are often compared to McCarthy's in their exploration of dark, bloody scenes and deformed or psychopathic characters—pushing the boundaries of knowledge is at the root of the grotesque. The reader might ask: Why would an author be so focused on vicious murderers, scalpers, rapists, thieves, and deformed, broken, and shredded or crushed bodies?

O'Connor replies that what is considered grotesque is exactly at the boundary between what we know and what we

Flannery O'Connor explored the world of the grotesque in her novels and short stories.

don't know, between here and over there, between what makes sense and what is a mystery. We think we're human and totally self-contained, until we encounter a dead body, a corpse. When we look at a corpse, we're reminded—very suddenly and sometimes to the point of nausea—that we ourselves are walking corpses. The mystery of consciousness and life is shown to us in death. All this is to say, O'Connor believes that violence and the grotesque have a place in fiction, and that does not have to be considered excessive or gratuitous. It is meaningful.

When we discuss the gnosticism that is being explored in *Blood Meridian*, we will revisit the concept of mystery and its importance to McCarthy. Mystery is what we might call meaningful ignorance, a kind of unknowing that has its own power or truth. As the West was mapped, explored, developed into cities and oil fields and plantations and mines, as the mysterious landscape was shaped into a grid, Americans had the sense that they were uncovering the secrets of the earth. But McCarthy—and O'Connor, in her own way—seems to be suggesting that this enlightenment of science, engineering, and government (which included the annihilation of the Native Americans) was built on a false knowledge and that the truth remained clouded in the mysteries of violence and death. Death, if you think about it, can't be understood fully from a scientific perspective since it can't be directly experienced, except finally and irrevocably.

Violence Is Sacred

But beyond being meaningful, in the fiction of O'Connor and McCarthy, violence is sacred. How could this be? At first violence seems paired with evil, where sacred seems paired with good. Wouldn't saying that violence is sacred be like saying that dark is light? Not necessarily. If we stick with the idea for a moment, it comes into focus. Light and dark exist in a duality, which means that neither exists without the other. Light and dark exist because they are different from each other, and some philosophers would argue that difference is itself the basis for all identity. Each thing is itself because it's not something else. But the relationship between violence and the sacred is not the same as the duality of light and dark. Violence is evil, let's assume, but if the sacred is the thing that is meant to redeem or provide salvation, then the sacred requires something bad to happen in order to bring us from the bad to the good. That's the definition of *redeem* in this context.

Two good examples from world religion: Christianity and Hinduism. In Hinduism, which is a very complex and rich religion that cannot be easily reduced, there are three main deities or sacred figures, called a trimurti, or trinity: Brahma the creator, Vishnu the preserver, and Shiva the destroyer. Each of the three is required and plays a critical function in the life and death of the universe; they represent a cycle of existence in which birth, life, and death are essential parts. The violence of Shiva is as essential as the creations of Brahma. Just so in the Christian tradition: In order for Christian mythology to function, Jesus of Nazareth had to be brutally tortured and executed, at which point he could be resurrected. The holy birth of Jesus, his violent death, and then his rebirth, are all essential parts of the sacred order in Christian belief.

So McCarthy is saying that violence is justified, in a certain sense. It is at the center of the story of sacred divinity. Evil is justified as well; every hero needs a villain. The problem is, while O'Connor writes from an explicitly Catholic Christian perspective and wants violence to be a redemptive force in her stories, McCarthy does not always follow this path. Frequently

FLANNERY O'CONNOR AND THE MOMENT OF GRACE

Flannery O'Connor's fiction has had a deep impact on American literature by blending religious themes with violence and dark humor. O'Connor is often regarded as one of the best American fiction writers, despite having her life cut short, at the age of thirty-nine, by the debilitating autoimmune disease lupus. She produced two novels and several collections of short stories.

O'Connor's tales take place in the American South, which she does not portray generously. That is, many of the characters she crafts are ugly, inside and out, or are marked by disease, mental instability, or some form of physical deformity. The societies that these characters inhabit are no more beautiful. But through all this unsavory haze, O'Connor always comes back to the question of religious faith, and particularly the Roman Catholic faith. Her interest was depicting the struggle, both internal and external, of the human soul to reconcile itself with a divine force in what she called a "moment of grace." One way to read her fiction is to look for the moment of grace, which for some characters is a revelation before dying, but for others is a mysterious or momentous shift in consciousness, like an epiphany or a sudden jolt. This peculiarly dark mixture of violence and religion makes O'Connor and McCarthy literary cousins.

in McCarthy's work, there are villains and then more villains. In essentially every one of his novels, violence doesn't redeem anyone. It's just there, it just happens, and it transcends human understanding. For this reason, McCarthy is absolutely in line with O'Connor: He is very much attuned to the mystery of existence, and the fact that violence exposes it. Some of O'Connor's works, such as her famous short story "A Good Man is Hard to Find," in which a serial killer murders a family in the woods, also seem to treat violence as something that will continue rather than being redeemed through the sacred. As critic Tim Parrish puts it, "Readers . . . prefer to see the kid [main character from McCarthy's *Blood Meridian*] and the grandmother [main character from "A Good Man is Hard to Find"] as representatives of some sort of redemption, which somehow washes away the sins of the killers. Shielding our eyes from the killer, without whom the meaning of redemption could not occur, we walk with our martyred characters towards God's shining light."[3] So even in the face of extreme killing and maiming, we readers are tempted to think that violence is always sacred and thus always redemptive. Reading *Blood Meridian* in particular, we should be careful of that temptation, since it will prove difficult to justify.

We can see the philosophy of sacred violence in a scene from *Blood Meridian* in which the judge (one of the major characters of the novel) declares that "each man's destiny is as large as the world he inhabits and contains within it all opposites as well. This desert upon which so many have been broken is vast and calls for largeness of heart, but it is also ultimately empty. It is hard, it is barren. Its very nature is stone."[4] The judge understands that there is a difference between oneness—everyone's destiny is the world, along with all the opposites therein—and some kind of substantial meaning.

To say that "all is one" sounds very meaningful and profound, but you might also say that "all is emptiness." The two statements don't contradict each other. In other words, the judge is saying we might all be part of a great oneness, and at the same time there might not be some ultimate meaning to that world unity.

"War Is the Ultimate Game": *Blood Meridian*

*B*lood Meridian, or the Evening Redness in the West* is based on a number of historical sources. Or, rather, there are events and characters in the book that resemble actual events and people, but the novel itself isn't properly historical fiction. The main difference between this novel and historical fiction is its purpose: It does not seem that the purpose of the text is to depict historical events "as they might have been" in order to educate or enlighten the reader. There doesn't seem to be a central lesson or moral framework for the novel at all. McCarthy takes the history of the Glanton gang and Judge Holden and makes them even *less* meaningful than most histories might. This relationship to history underscores the novel's main theme, which is that existence does not function according to human logic nor to moral reason; there is simply life and death and everything that comes between. The life and death of humans is much the same as the life and death of any organism, and violence is as meaningless as kindness.

The Glanton Gang and Scalp-Hunting

Despite the novel's suggestion that history is not a human endeavor and cannot be understood in human terms, the book does have quite a bit of historical material embedded in it. At its core, the book tells of the bloody exploits of Captain John Joel Glanton along the Mexico–Texas border during the years 1848 to 1850. Like "the kid" who is one of the major characters

An artist's rendering of the first battle of the Mexican–American War. In *Blood Meridian*, it is this conflict that shaped Glanton, the novel's main character.

of the novel, Glanton was in the business of war by the time he was sixteen. He fought in a number of campaigns that the United States was waging against Mexico in the years leading up to 1848, known as the Mexican–American War. The United States wanted to negotiate for a border that followed the Rio Grande (which is where the United States–Mexico border is currently), and they wanted to take over territory that is now Arizona, New Mexico, and California, along with Texas. But Mexico, understandably, resisted giving up its territory, so US President James Polk sent in troops to enforce the matter.

When the war ended, there were still men bent on murder (and, as the novel tells us, there always will be). Beginning in 1849, when the war had officially ended and the military had withdrawn, Glanton led a gang of mercenaries through the northern Mexican states of Chihuahua and Sonora. His mission was to rid the territory of Apache Indians who raided the towns and villages there, so his contract with the Mexican states' governments was to bring back Apache Indian scalps as proof that the mercenaries had killed the Indians. Each scalp would net the mercenaries a certain amount of money. Because of this economic incentive, Glanton and his men took to killing not only the Indians but any defenseless Mexican villagers they could find, since the scalps couldn't easily be differentiated. Once word of these massacres spread, Glanton was driven out of Mexico. He and his gang traveled to what is now southwestern Arizona, on the border with California, to the Colorado River where some Yuma Indians were operating a profitable ferry business.

This was the time of the California Gold Rush, drawing new settlers and gold prospectors (the '49ers, now the name of the National Football League [NFL] team in San Francisco), so anyone traveling north from Mexico into California would

Civil War soldier, artist, and author Samuel Chamberlain. His account of the Mexican–American War is the primary source for McCarthy's *Blood Meridian*.

cross the river there, and the ferryboat owners charged them a fee for safe passage. Glanton took forcible control of one ferryboat (owned by Dr. A. L. Lincoln, relative of future President Abraham Lincoln) and began the even more profitable business of murdering travelers and taking everything they had. Glanton's men sabotaged and killed the Yuma Indians who operated the rival ferry downriver. In retaliation, the Yuma attacked Glanton's camp, killing him and his crew, ending their reign of terror. Unfortunately for the Yuma (also known as Quechan), this action against Glanton, while justified from their perspective, also instigated a decade-long campaign by the California government to wipe out the Indians. The killing never stopped.

Sources for Glanton's Story

Much of what is known about the Glanton gang comes from a single source: a book written by one of the participants, Samuel E. Chamberlain, fittingly called *My Confession: The Recollections of a Rogue*. It's a vibrant and often historically inaccurate (but exciting!) account of Chamberlain's time in the US Army fighting in Mexico, and then his subsequent involvement with Glanton. Characters from McCarthy's novel, which seem like they must be fictional given their demonic qualities, appear already formed in Chamberlain's text. Glanton himself is there, of course, but the star is Judge Holden. Chamberlain describes him as over six feet tall, and "a cooler blooded villain never went unhung." He spoke numerous languages and was well-acquainted with geology and mineralogy, an excellent marksman, and, crucially, hairless. The judge's sexual aggression is also present in Chamberlain's story: A young girl was found violated and strangled, with the bruise of a very large hand around her throat. No one ever accused the judge directly, however.[1]

Other sources that McCarthy must have drawn from include David Lavender's 1954 narrative history *Bent's Fort* and John C. Cremony's 1868 firsthand account *Life Among the Apaches,* in which Glanton is referred to as John Gallantin. "This man," writes Cremony, "had the reputation of being one of the worst scoundrels who ever existed even in that demoralized and villainous region."[2] When the Yuma murder Glanton and his crew, Cremony declares it "his well-merited fate."[3] Beyond the specifics of Glanton's death, Cremony provides historical weight to the almost unbelievable violence of McCarthy's book, which one might assume is just exaggerated, literary imagination. But Cremony tells us otherwise:

> At the period about which I am writing, Arizona and New Mexico were cursed by the presence of two or three hundred of the most infamous scoundrels it is possible to conceive. Innocent and unoffending men were shot down or bowie-knived merely for the pleasure of witnessing their death agonies. Men walked the streets and public squares with double-barreled shot guns, and hunted each other as sportsmen hunt for game.[4]

This is the American West before it became a mythic place of redemption and heroism in the Western literary and cinematic genre. *Blood Meridian* digs deep to a time when violence was just the way of things. By subverting the Hollywood image of virtuous cowboys, the novel also helps us rethink contemporary violence and war. It poses the question: Is American violence justifiable when it seems to uphold white superiority, patriotism, and the mythology of white male heroism?

This painting by Samuel Chamberlain depicts the Battle of Buena Vista during the Mexican–American War.

Blood Meridian: Plot and Characters

The novel begins with the command, "See the child." This is the character known only as "the kid" (and near the end of the text, "the man"). The kid's mother dies in childbirth and his father is an alcoholic. He leaves home at the age of fourteen to join the filibuster gangs fighting for the United States in the wars with Mexico along the border. The first part of the novel ends with the kid being one of only a handful of survivors of a bloody encounter with the Apache Indians. From this, we get a glimpse of the full depths to which the novel will take us into blood and gore, and the clinical descriptions of dismemberment and assault that men (not women, in this text) are driven to exact on anyone in their way.

The kid joins up with John Glanton's gang, and their reign of terror across the borderlands takes up the majority of the novel. As in the historical reality, the Glanton gang marauds its way along Chihuahua and Sonora. We meet several colorful and unusual characters, including Toadvine, one of the kid's early friends, who is distinguished for having no ears (they were cut off his head in some earlier episode), Glanton himself, who is vicious and seems to have no conscience, and Judge Holden (also known simply as "the judge"), who comes to serve as the second central character of the novel. The judge is special in a number of ways. He is described as being seven feet tall, completely bald, no hair on his face—not even eyebrows or eyelashes—and built like a mountain. He can speak any language (it seems—he converses in English, German, Spanish, and several Indian languages), claims never to sleep, and also claims that he will never die. He can dance gracefully and plays a masterful fiddle. He knows archaeology like a professor, and argues like a lawyer. And the judge is the cruelest killer of them all. In the book he embodies total and perpetual war. After the gang is devastated by a group of Yuma Indians, the judge confronts the kid, kills him in an outhouse, and dances the night away as the only surviving member of the gang.

The Hero Who Learns a Lesson

Insofar as heroes learn a lesson, the hero is the kid, although as we think about this novel, that is a difficult statement to uphold. The kid does become "the man" by the end, and he heroically stands up to the judge in their final scenes. But the kid's world is not redeemed through his growth. He simply survives until he himself is murdered. Just before encountering the judge at the end, the man guns down a young teenager who tries to kill him at his camp outside of town. This slaughter symbolizes the man killing his former self, but it is not satisfying in that way. The teenager he shoots is survived by a younger boy, his brother "the orphan."

> Randall you take a good look at the man that has made you an orphan.

> The orphan in his large clothes holding the old musket with the mended stock stared at him woodenly. He was maybe twelve years old and he looked not so much dull-witted as insane . . .[5]

And after the other boys collect the dead boy's belongings and carry his body away, the orphan

> did not assist as a bearer for he was too small. When they set out across the prairie with his brother's body carried up on their shoulders he followed behind carrying the musket and the dead boy's rifle and the dead boy's hat. The man watched them go. Out there was nothing. They

were simply bearing the body off over the bonestrewn waste toward a naked horizon. The orphan turned once to look back at him and then he hurried to catch up.[6]

The dead boy, then, doesn't really serve a symbolic purpose. Instead of being redeemed by the violence of their encounter, the body is just being carried out into "nothing," "bonestrewn waste," a "naked horizon." The orphan story might be the beginning of a heroic Western tale of revenge, but it won't be. It will only be a continuation of the bloody episodes that the kid has lived through. No real lessons have been learned, and nothing has changed.

Interpreting *Blood Meridian*: "The Mystery Is That There Is No Mystery"

Blood Meridian tells this tale of killing and wandering without really seeming to argue that the actions of the characters are good or bad. This is, probably, what makes the novel so disturbing. As modern readers, we are used to being given a narrative that helps us understand the moral crisis and how it should be decided. In other words, we expect to find a core conflict, and then read how the conflict is resolved. When we learn to read and interpret literature, we often encounter lists of conflicts and their categories: conflicts between two individuals, between an individual and society at large, between two societies, between an individual and nature, and so on. *Blood Meridian* doesn't offer up any sort of literary conflict that we, as readers, can understand as meaningful. As literary critic Dana Phillips puts it, "traditional concepts of the narrator as a 'person' or 'voice . . . ' with an interest in certain 'themes' that help to structure the text, do not apply to *Blood Meridian*."[7] While the novel is narrated from an omniscient perspective, "there seems to be no knower providing us with the knowledge it imparts. And this knowledge does not really develop; it merely accrues."[8] Events just sort of pile up, one after the other: comic, pathetic, ugly, natural, human, or animal. Events do not seem to surround a theme, and nothing seems to be more important than anything else. Phillips again: "The novel does not seek to resolve 'conflicts' which trouble its characters, much less its narrator or author. It is not really a narrative, then, but a description—and some would say it is not really a novel either."[9]

This makes the book difficult to interpret the way we would normally go about interpreting a text, since we tend to assume that there is some message to be read among the events, characters, and words of the story. For all its spectacular violence and intricate language, there is something unnervingly empty about *Blood Meridian* that leaves the reader feeling drained and uncertain at the end. It explodes the very idea of novels having a purpose or saying something. This novel just says what it says, and the events are as they are, and what meaning there is to be found is on a larger scale than the individual lives of the characters. By extension, *Blood Meridian* could be suggesting that the meaning of any individual life, including our own, can't really be resolved in the way we want to believe, and that life and death are a series of soft vibrations in a massive, complex universal symphony that we will never be able to hear.

The Mysteries of Gnosticism in *Blood Meridian*

Several scholars have pointed out that McCarthy is expressing a peculiar kind of philosophy in this novel, a sort of religious philosophy known as gnosticism. *Gnosis* is a Greek word that is usually translated as "knowledge," although in the context of the gnostic religious beliefs, it can be understood as enlightenment or spiritual knowledge. Gnosticism is not an organized religion like Christianity or Islam, but it has emerged in various forms through many cultures and time periods. The basic belief system relies on the idea that the material world is a prison, and that the spiritual world or the world of the soul is a place of freedom from physical constraints. In relation to Christianity, gnostic belief holds that the God of Abraham (the God of the Old Testament) is a demiurge, an evil creator who has imprisoned human souls in imperfect bodies. In the myth of the Garden of Eden, it is the snake who is punished for tempting Eve to eat the fruit from the Tree of the Knowledge of Good and Evil. The snake is punished, in other words, for giving Adam and Eve gnosis. The one who wants to keep them in ignorance is God, whom the gnostics say is evil and must be resisted. The serpent therefore represents true knowledge and freedom.

How does gnosticism operate in *Blood Meridian*? There are numerous references to the impossibility of knowing, for example. In an early nocturnal encounter with a solitary old man on a desolate plain, the kid is sitting with the man at a measly camp fire.

> The old man swung his head back and forth. The way of the transgressor is hard. God made this world, but he didnt make it to suit everbody, did he?
>
> I dont believe he much had me in mind.
>
> Aye, said the old man. But where does a man come by his notions. What world's he seen that he liked better?
>
> I can think of better places and better ways.
>
> Can ye make it be?

No.

No. It's a mystery. A man's at odds to know his mind cause his mind is aught he has to know it with. He can know his heart, but he dont want to. Rightly so. Best not to look in there. It aint the heart of a creature that is bound in the way that God has set for it. You can find meanness in the least of creatures, but when God made man the devil was at his elbow. A creature that can do anything. Make a machine. And a machine to make the machine. And evil that can run itself a thousand years, no need to tend it. You believe that?

I dont know.

Believe that.[10]

The early Christian gnostics believed that God was an evil, imperfect creator who had created an evil, imperfect world. Knowledge of the ultimate goodness of the world is contained in a mysterious, cosmic force beyond the material world, according to this line of thought. The old man is pointing out that not only is the world unknowable, but one's own mind is unknowable, since the knowledge produced by an imperfect creation—the human mind—is subject to its own imperfections. Is goodness possible? Is the world entirely evil? It's impossible to say. But what is true, he says, is that a human being is the ultimate evil, a creation on which the devil himself consulted. Humans are made in God's image in the sense that they, too, are capable of evil creations. The kid admits, however, that he doesn't know what to believe.

Later in the novel, when the judge is preaching his strange philosophies to the Glanton gang around another campfire in another wasteland, he notes that "Even in this world more things exist without our knowledge than with it and the order in creation which you see is that which you have put there, like a string in a maze, so that you shall not lose your way. For existence has its own order and that no man's mind can compass, that mind itself being but a fact among others."[11] This is a reflection of the old man's warning that we think we know ourselves as human beings, but our so-called knowledge is just an illusion. We have created knowledge, but the true order of existence goes beyond our capability to know. What we do know, though, is that humans wage war; war is "the ultimate trade awaiting its ultimate practitioner."[12]

During the same discussion, the judge notes that what is right and true will ultimately crumble, and have to be judged according to a higher law:

> Man's vanity may well approach the infinite in capacity but his knowledge remains imperfect and howevermuch he comes to value his judgements ultimately he must submit them before a higher court. Here there can be no special pleading. Here are considerations of equity and rectitude and moral right rendered void and without warrant and here are the views of the litigants despised. Decisions of life and death, of what shall be and what shall not, beggar all question of right.[13]

Again, the judge echoes the old man in his indictment of humanity as having the capacity for infinite vanity, infinite self-centeredness. These speeches also echo Ecclesiastes, the book of Old Testament teachings that declare that "all is vanity"[14] and that "however much man may toil in seeking, he will not find it out. Even though a wise man claims to know, he cannot find it out."[15] That profound and poetic book of the Bible also maintains that good or bad alike will return to the dust from which they came, and that it is vanity (or, illusory) to think that because you are wise you might escape this fate. Everyone dies.

There are a number of formulations like this that express the notion that what we hope to know about the world and about ourselves as human beings can ultimately be reduced to a few universal concepts: war, violence, death, and then nothingness. We can read this as a form of gnosticism because it criticizes the idea that we can somehow redeem ourselves in life. Life, according to the gnostics, is a form of imprisonment in the body—freedom is really only possible through death. This philosophy that leads to death is unnerving and disquieting, to say the least, but it insists that by rejecting the possibility of winning the game of life (no one, you might say, gets to take their wealth with them) and embracing mystery, we allow the possibility of accessing true spiritual knowledge.

The Game of Life and Death

In a review for the *Los Angeles Times*, Eric Miles Williamson suggests that *No Country for Old Men*, McCarthy's first novel published after the Border Trilogy, is a return to the "problem of evil" that McCarthy explored in *Blood Meridian*. And while the setting has been updated from the mid-nineteenth century to the 1980s, "one would like to think we have become more civilized over the course of 130 years. According to McCarthy, we have not. In fact, we have gotten worse."[16] This tale of hit men, cartels, stolen cash, and old-school lawmen, is, as Williamson notes, on the surface a gangster novel. But with McCarthy's characteristic strangeness and philosophical depth, it speaks to something more than just good versus bad, law and lawlessness, and wonders about the very nature of being human.

A 1968 photograph captures the aftermath of a battle during the Vietnam War. Some argue that McCarthy's treatment of war themes in *Blood Meridian* was influenced by the violence of Vietnam.

Is *Blood Meridian* a Novel About Vietnam?

A soldier wears a necklace of human body parts as trophies of war. Entire villages are destroyed in fire, gun smoke, and bloody blades. And the American perpetrators of this catastrophe were invited there to defend their political ideals against a hostile superpower. These are all fair descriptions of both *Blood Meridian* and the Vietnam War. Several critics have noted the correspondence between the novel and the disastrous war in Southeast Asia that took place between 1955 and 1975. Vince Brewton, in an article published in the *Southern Literary Journal*, argues forcefully that Vietnam "left a deep imprint on [McCarthy's] early work." In addition to the influence of the war on McCarthy's themes, "*Blood Meridian* comes close to being a novel whose true subject is Vietnam, a kind of allegory of American involvement in Southeast Asia and of the reverberations of that history in the American psyche."[17]

Does this analysis hold up? It might. Besides the obvious political similarities between the American incursion into Mexico and the American intervention in Vietnam, both in the name of freedom and democracy, the structure of violence is strangely similar. For example, the American strategy during the Vietnam War was based on the theory of attrition: If the United States could kill enough North Vietnamese people, it would outlast them, and thus win. In order to measure this progress, the US military kept careful statistical logs, based in large part on body counts. In the end, it didn't matter who exactly was killed—men, women, the elderly, children—as much as how many. On March 16, 1968, a group of American soldiers entered a small village in Vietnam and killed, raped, and mutilated between 347 and 504 Vietnamese women, children, and elderly men and women. This became known as the My Lai Massacre. The details of the event closely match the scenes of total destruction that the Glanton gang bring down on Mexican villages, in which the mercenaries don't care whom they kill—young or old, innocent or guilty, Apache or Mexican—so long as they increase their scalp count.

While there are a number of interesting themes in this text, we should focus on one in particular that links *No Country* with *Blood Meridian*: the idea that life and existence is a game with rules that are either incomprehensible or uncontrollable by human beings.

In *Blood Meridian*, the judge explores this theme explicitly during one of his fireside sermons. In it, he justifies his view that war is the most elemental condition of the universe, a condition that is at the heart of existence itself. To explain this idea to his uneducated companions, the judge first notes that "men are born for games. Nothing else. Every child knows that play is nobler than work."[18] What is valuable about a game, asks the judge, other than the stakes? And the ultimate stakes are life and death. "Games of chance require a wager to have meaning at all," he notes, and with games of skill you risk the "humiliation of defeat" and you might win "the pride of victory."[19] But he concludes that "trial of chance or trial of worth all games aspire to the condition of war for here that which is wagered swallows up game, player, all."[20] In other words, the most important game is the game of life and death, which the judge imagines as a card game between two men who have "nothing to wager save their lives." When life and death are on the table, we can see clearly that war is a game, and all games are versions of war:

> . . .War is the truest form of divination. It is the testing of one's will and the will of another within that larger will which because it binds them is therefore forced to select. War is the ultimate game because war is at last a forcing of the unity of existence. War is god.[21]

We find meaning in war, according to the judge, in the contest of wills that ends in life and death. And in that contest, two things are forced together to determine what exists and what will disappear. The process of war is the process of making and unmaking, which is the function of a god.

In the final scene of *Blood Meridian*, the kid (now the man) has spent twenty-eight years wandering after his experience with the Glanton gang, and he has finally crossed paths with the judge, who appears not to have aged at all. The judge has a long conversation with the kid at a bar (before murdering him in an outhouse), and the conversation turns once more on morality, evil, life, and death. But the idea of games emerges once more, and it is a useful contrast to what will happen in *No Country for Old Men*. As the judge sermonizes to the kid, he returns to the theme of worshiping war as a god:

> A ritual includes the letting of blood. Rituals which fail in this requirement are but mock rituals. Here every man knows the false at once. Never doubt it. That feeling in the breast that evokes a child's memory of loneliness such as when the others have gone and only the game is left with its solitary participant. A solitary game, without opponent. Where only the rules are at hazard. Dont look away. We are not speaking in mysteries. You of all men are no stranger to that feeling, the emptiness and the despair. It is that which we take arms against, is it not? Is not blood the tempering agent in the mortar which bonds?[22]

Here the game is a ritual without any central meaning, without an opponent. If war is at the heart of everything, then an opponent is required. Similarly, if rituals are a form of worshiping violence, then they must include "the letting of blood." By this way of thinking, what the Glanton gang was doing—scalping, murdering, wantonly destroying— was a kind of pious prayer to the true god who is war. Blood

Javier Bardem stars as Anton Chigurh in the 2007 film adaptation of *No Country for Old Men*. In the story, Chigurh decides whether his victim will live or die by the flip of a coin.

is the "tempering agent," the substance that makes mortar hold together and binds two bricks. It is the stuff that holds the universe together, McCarthy is saying, stuff that is required for life and is let loose in death. Blood has been invoked as a defining feature, throughout history of family, nation, and race.

The Coin Flip of Life

"What's the most you ever lost on a coin toss?" asks Anton Chigurh, the psychopathic killer stalking the pages of *No Country for Old Men*. ("Chigurh" sounds like a play on the archaic word "chirurgeon," or, surgeon.) Early in the novel he is standing in a gas station in a remote desert town, and the clerk is very clearly unnerved by Chigurh's presence. The reader knows that he is capable of killing this man in an instant, but Chigurh is driven by what he believes is an inexorable fate. He asks the man to call the coin toss: heads or tails.

> You need to call it, Chigurh said. I cant call it for you. It wouldnt be fair. It wouldnt even be right. Just call it.

> I didnt put nothin up.

> Yes you did. You've been putting it up your whole life. You just didnt know it. You know what the date is on this coin?

> No.

> It's nineteen fifty-eight. It's been traveling twenty-two years to get here. And now it's here. And I'm here. And I've got my hand over it. And it's either heads or tails. And you have to say. Call it.

> I dont know what it is I stand to win.

In the blue light the man's face was beaded thinly with sweat. He licked his upper lip.

You stand to win everything, Chigurh said. Everything.

You aint makin any sense, mister.

Call it.

Heads then.

Chigurh uncovered the coin. He turned his arm slightly for the man to see. Well done, he said.[23]

The dialogue is not involved, and there is no narrative description; the characters seem rooted to their spots, unmoving. This creates enormous tension. Will Chigurh kill the shopkeeper? It hinges on the coin flip. Life and death hangs in the balance, but the contest is not even between two people anymore, it is simply a question of chance. Chigurh is only the dark messenger, as it were, of fate itself. He is the epitome of the judge's quest for violence since all human quality has disappeared from the enactment of death.

THE BORDER TRILOGY

Poet, teacher, and cultural critic Gloria Anzaldúa was born and grew up near the Texas border with Mexico. In 1987 she published a book of semiautobiographical essays and poems, written in a blend of different dialects of Spanish and English, titled *Borderlands/La Frontera*. In its opening pages, she paints a moving picture of that border that she had known since her childhood:

> The U.S-Mexican border es *una herida abierta* where the Third World grates against the first and bleeds. And before a scab forms it hemorrhages again, the lifeblood of two worlds merging to form a third country—a border culture. Borders are set up to define the places that are safe and unsafe, to distinguish *us* from *them*. A border is a dividing line, a narrow strip along a steep edge. A borderland is a vague and undetermined place created by the emotional residue of an unnatural boundary. It is in a constant state of transition. The prohibited and forbidden are its inhabitants . . . The only "legitimate" inhabitants are those in power, the whites and those who align themselves with whites. Tension grips the inhabitants of the borderlands like a virus. Ambivalence and unrest reside there and death is no stranger.[1]

"Una herida abierta" is an open wound. Anzaldúa sees the border as a bleeding gash, a place of violence where the blood of two cultures mixes to form a third. But the border

Mexican children play near a fence that stands at the border of the United States and Mexico. This bleak landscape is the setting for McCarthy's three novels known as the Border Trilogy: *All the Pretty Horses*, *The Crossing*, and *Cities of the Plain*.

is not defined by fences or walls, which are static and solid. Borders, for Anzaldúa, are "vague and undetermined" and "in a constant state of transition." The borderlands are tense, full of power struggles, unrest, prohibition, danger, and death.

Cormac McCarthy's Border Trilogy is precisely about this violent line drawn in the earth that marks the official national boundaries between the United States and Mexico, but also the metaphorical boundary between life and death, between youth and old age, between innocence and knowledge, between heaven and hell. The image of humanity that McCarthy paints in these three novels is, by turns, bleak and uplifting, but he is consistently ambivalent about quick and easy answers to the important questions of life and death that his characters face. His ambivalence is a reflection of the border itself, just as Anzaldúa described it. Disaster seems to stalk McCarthy's protagonists, and while a reader might expect to understand the stories by their good-versus-evil arrangements, McCarthy almost never gives us the satisfaction of knowing where evil comes from or who is responsible for it. Evil, as we have already seen in McCarthy's work, seems to simply *be there*, waiting for us to stumble on it, with disastrous consequences.

We are also treated to an amazing display of heroism in the Border Trilogy, but it is ultimately a brutal and empty heroism, usually with no tangible reward except lonely survival. John Grady Cole and Billy Parham, the two cowboys who star in the trilogy, each make a painful transition from boy to man. They each face violent challenges and death with almost holy resolve, and their characters are intimately bound up in their relationship to animals.

Mythic Places

In a chapter called "Dire Cartographies" from her book *In Other Worlds: Science Fiction and the Human Imagination*, renowned novelist Margaret Atwood argues that the imagination of otherness, of what is horrifying or dangerous, tends to occur at the edges of the map. "With every map there's an edge," she writes, "a border between the known and the unknown," and it is the unknown that produces fear.[2] As Western civilization and science progressively explored and uncovered the landscapes of the planet, this knowledge pushed the "edge of the map" progressively outward, until science fiction took hold and began to set stories in space, beyond the terrestrial map altogether. Maps are analogies for security, safety, and structured knowledge. Literature uses maps to explore dark zones, and imagine what monsters might lurk there. "In literature, every landscape is a state of mind, but every state of mind can also be portrayed by a landscape."[3] Thus, with Cormac McCarthy, and in particular with a trilogy of novels named after a cartographic feature—the border—we have to be attuned to the potential meanings and cultural significance of what's *here* and what's *there*.

Critics of McCarthy have pointed out that his so-called Mexican novels, which would include the Border Trilogy as well as *Blood Meridian* and *No Country for Old Men*, use Mexico as an otherworldly location where a white hero might wander, as if he is visiting an alien planet, off the edge of the map. The question is: Does McCarthy unfairly portray Mexico? After all, for people who live there, Mexico is normal and every day, and the United States would be foreign. A number of American and European authors have also portrayed Mexico as a kind of underworld or alien place, as a strange wilderness or as culturally primitive and magical. This representational strategy is sometimes referred to as the "Infernal Paradise" myth, which is used by Anglo-European writers as a foil for its white heroes. As Daniel Cooper Alarcón puts it, a literary work's authenticity has become based on its inclusion of the Infernal Paradise myth, which marks Mexico as "enchanting/repellent, beautiful/desolate, civilized/cruel, dreamlike/bloody, [and] paradisal/infernal."[4] McCarthy seems to uphold these literary dichotomies, and his "Mexican novels fit neatly within the Infernal Paradise tradition, doing little to challenge its assumptions and conventions."[5]

> **dichotomy**
>
> A contrast or an opposition between two things, such as religion and science, or dark and light.

> **foil**
>
> A character or object that is used in a narrative to highlight qualities in a different character.

> **trajectory**
>
> A way of describing the movement of a story.

Epics, Ancient and Modern

Each of the novels can be read and appreciated separately, but the three books as a trilogy tell an epic. In order to understand the scope and themes of the stories, we should try to determine what genres these novels fit into, if any at all. McCarthy's work, as we saw in Chapter 2, with the difficulty of applying the term Southern Gothic, is hard to classify. Epic is a broader genre of literature since it appears in many different forms, times, and places, but it might be a more useful categorization of McCarthy's work in general. An epic is a story that has a wide scope, that attempts to conjure an entire world in the course of its telling, and that tends to

Homer's *Odyssey*, illustrated here by painter William Turner, is a classic epic tale that follows the hero as he embarks on a quest. Similarly, McCarthy's Border Trilogy follows the protagonists on their own journeys of growth and knowledge.

follow one or more heroic characters on their quest. Traditionally, an epic is a long poem. *The Odyssey* by Homer is a classic example of an epic. *The Epic of Gilgamesh* was composed even earlier than Homer's Greek tales, and certain stories from the Old and New Testament could also fit the epic framework. In a more modern way, the Western genre—with cowboys, shootouts, and train robbers—is structured around an epic trajectory.

This is precisely where Cormac McCarthy's work fits. McCarthy's characters are from the American wilderness—the Appalachian Mountains or the deserts of the Southwest—and even as they are more or less Western style characters with their revolvers and horses, McCarthy relies heavily on ancient symbols to give his work a distinctive, sinister edge. In other words, the novels strike a balance between modern settings (nineteenth- and twentieth-century North America) and a sense of ancient evil.

The Hero's Journey

The most important element of an epic, however, is its structure as a hero's journey or quest narrative. As Gail Moore Morrison puts it,

> . . . most of McCarthy's novels, despite their apparent episodic organization, involve both metaphoric and literal journeys which bring their voyages inevitably into a series of conflicts and confrontations with themselves as well as with the various communities intersected by their wanderings. And, in most of these novels, the central characters' journeys, however random in time and place they may be, are apparently rooted in dysfunctional families and troubled filial relationships.[6]

The hero's journey is usually both a metaphoric and literal journey, as Morrison notes. The hero, an extraordinary person with certain powers, receives a quest that takes him away from his home. While on his quest, he faces hardship and danger. Overcoming these obstacles, he gains what he was seeking, and returns home. When he returns home, the hero has not only brought a prize—the object of his quest—but he has brought wisdom, which he shares with his culture. This cycle of home-away-home is replayed in countless narratives beginning from the very birth of literature and storytelling.

The ancient Greeks were interested in conveying the ritual importance of the hero's journey, which they expressed as a metaphorical movement from life to death and back, from innocence to knowledge, or from youth to adulthood. The ritual of transition through the hero's journey is a common feature in much of Western literature, but it is particularly important to the Border Trilogy. According to the heroic pattern, an extraordinary man (usually a man, unfortunately) is given a quest that will take him away from his home; he visits dark, dangerous lands in search of the resolution to his mission; he returns home at the end, a concept the Greeks called *nostos* (literally "homecoming"), armed with new knowledge and new experience to restore order and reset the cycle.

The Hero "Comes of Age"

The cycle of heroism from ancient literature maps onto the Border novels, but not without being invested with McCarthy's signature rejection of neat reduction to stock forms. For example, *All the Pretty Horses* is on the surface a fairly straightforward *bildungsroman* that charts John Grady Cole's transition from boy to man, from naive innocence to a truth-seeker, across the border between human and animal, and geographically from his home in Texas south to Mexico and back. The movement south is an allegory of the descent to the underworld, which is a typical destination for ancient heroes in search of the meaning of life. Why not visit the place of death itself?

> **bildungsroman**
>
> A novel that has to do with a young person growing up, developing, or coming of age.

The Crossing is even more suffused with this allegorical movement; Billy Parham makes the crossing from the United States to Mexico multiple times, and plays with a similarly fuzzy boundary between man and animal. Billy's various

In *All the Pretty Horses*, two best friends, John Grady Cole and Lacey
Rawlins (played by Matt Damon and Henry Thomas in the film),
set out for Mexico in order to find work as cowboys.

quests are emblematic of the ancient hero: He wants to restore the natural world by relocating a wolf; he travels with his brother to recapture some horses stolen from their family ranch; and in a final, devastating quest, Billy goes alone to find his brother, only to find him dead.

Cities of the Plain, while less philosophically rich than the previous two novels, is necessary to sustain the arc of epic and heroic metaphor, because it intertwines Billy's and John Grady's stories in a final attempt for both to find something meaningful in life. After John Grady's "heroic" death in a knife fight, it is Billy who is left to grapple with the remains of life that seems tragic. In a final episode, Billy meets Death himself under a highway underpass. He escapes and the trilogy ends on a hopeful note, but without the complete restoration of truth and justice that characterizes the typical ancient epic. McCarthy always resists the tidy resolution.

All the Pretty Horses

All the Pretty Horses is arguably Cormac McCarthy's most accessible book. It is surprising, though, since it tells a fairly conventional romantic tragedy (the boy meets the girl, but can't have the girl) on the one hand, and yet on the other, contains McCarthy's trademark darkness and weirdness. The story focuses on John Grady Cole, a teenage rancher from Texas who travels to Mexico with his childhood friend Lacey Rawlins. As with all three of the novels in this series, the crux of meaning has to do with crossing borders or transitioning/metamorphosing from one state to another.

Grady and Rawlins are both experienced cowboys by the time they are teenagers. After Grady's parents' divorce, he and Rawlins run away from home to look for work as cowboys in Mexico. Before they cross the border, they encounter a younger boy, just thirteen or fourteen, riding a magnificent black horse, who claims his name is Jimmy Blevins (the name of a well-known radio evangelist). The three boys ride into Mexico. Rawlins dislikes and distrusts Blevins immediately. Blevins's horse escapes during a violent thunderstorm, and Blevins is forced to steal it back from the Mexican villagers who found it. Blevins rides away with a posse of Mexicans at his heels, while Grady and Rawlins escape in a different direction, not wanting to be captured and accused of being horse thieves.

The two friends escape the Mexican townspeople and encounter a cowboy's paradise in the form of *La Purisima,* a cattle and horse ranch owned by Don Hector. The owner quickly realizes the two teenagers' skill at horse-breaking and herding. He hires Grady (more naturally talented than Rawlins) to manage the breeding of a new champion stallion he's purchased from the United States. During his work with the horses, Grady has a chance to fall in love with Alejandra, Don Hector's beautiful young daughter. She falls for him as well, and despite warnings from Rawlins and Dueña Alfonsa, Alejandra's powerful aunt, Grady begins a passionate affair with Alejandra, secretly meeting her in his room after dark. Some weeks later, a troop of police officers arrive and arrest Rawlins and Grady, and it is made clear that Don Hector was the one who turned them in, we suppose because he found out about Alejandra. They are reunited in jail with Blevins, who was captured after killing a Mexican man. The three boys are transported to a deserted location where an evil police captain executes Blevins. Grady and Rawlins end up in a penitentiary in Mexico, where they both must fight for their lives. John Grady kills an assassin in a knife fight, and Dueña Alfonsa finally purchases their freedom.

John Grady heads back to Texas with the horses he retrieved after kidnapping the police captain.

Once free from prison, Rawlins returns to Texas. John Grady is told that he cannot see Alejandra; these were the terms of his release from prison. He doesn't accept the terms and spends one final night with her. She tells him that she cannot be with him. In the end, he rescues the horses they first brought to Texas, including Blevins's huge black stallion. In a fit of revenge, Grady takes the police captain hostage and drags him across the desert, finally giving him up to local authorities for criminal prosecution. Grady wanders Texas vainly searching for Blevins's horse's owner. After a farewell to Rawlins, Grady rides off into the sunset.

Lack of Inner Worlds

In this novel, clues to the psychology of the main character, John Grady, are often withheld by the narrator. In typical, modern novels with omniscient narrators, the reader is given access to the inner workings of the characters' minds. Often, authors make this access explicit. For example, in another contemporary American novel by Jonathan Franzen, *Freedom*, we read about the protagonist's moral dilemma concerning his love for two women:

> Each new thing he encountered in life impelled him in a direction that fully convinced him of its rightness, but then the next new thing loomed up and impelled him in the opposite direction, which also felt right. There was no controlling narrative: he seemed to himself a purely reactive pinball in a game whose only object was to stay alive for staying alive's sake.[7]

From this passage, the reader is able to discern how the character feels about himself, and is given insight into his decision-making process. We see his waking psychology in action. For McCarthy's characters, however, this psychology is either not on display or it isn't there at all, which is probably why so many of these characters seem sociopathic or downright evil. In Grady's case, though, the lack of inner dialogue reinforces the sense that he is a "man among men" (a phrase used in *Blood Meridian*, the novel written just prior to *Pretty Horses*). We know that he is a passionate person from his behavior, but when he is required to face some danger or torment, or even to cope with the loss of Alejandra, he does so with grit and steely action. Dumped by his true love? First, get drunk and participate in a few bar fights. Second, stage a suicidal mission to single-handedly rescue three horses and take a Mexican police captain hostage.

Dreams and Dreamworlds

In keeping with McCarthy's reliance on a mysterious interplay between real and unreal, or between waking and dreaming, dreams play a key role in stitching together the world of *Pretty Horses*. The landscape itself appears as a dreamscape, a dream of the past. For example, in the first pages of the novel, John Grady has just seen his grandfather buried. He rides out "where he would always choose to ride,"

> At the hour he'd always choose when the shadows were long and the ancient road was shaped before him in the rose and canted light like a dream of the past where the painted ponies and the riders of the lost nation came down out of the north with their faces chalked and their long hair plaited and each armed for war which was their life and the women and children and women with children at their breasts all of them pledged in blood and redeemable in blood only.[8]

As he is riding, the ghostly daydream of Comanche riders—perhaps a nod to the events a century before depicted in *Blood Meridian*—emerges in the evening light. The dream tells a history—the eradication of Indian tribes and nations—and foreshadows the novel's trajectory—the requirement of blood and war to defend what each person values.

But the image of the hard, masculine exterior is softened somewhat by his dreams, which seem to weave together his honorable spirit with the American frontier and the horses that he rides so expertly. One dream Grady has late in the novel, while imprisoned by the sadistic police captain and awaiting whatever justice will be made available to him, is typical of the dream sequences in this novel. The dream is told in a single run-on sentence, bound together with parataxis:

> That night he dreamt of horses in a field on a high plain where the spring rains had brought up the grass and the wildflowers out of the ground and the flowers ran all blue and yellow far as the eye could see and in the dream he was among the horses running and in the dream he himself could run with the horses and they coursed the young mares and fillies over the plain where their rich bay and their rich chestnut colors shone in the sun and the young colts ran with their dams and trampled down the flowers in a haze of pollen that hung in the sun like powdered gold and they ran he and the horses out along the high mesas where the ground resounded under their running hooves and they flowed and changed and ran and their manes and tails blew off of them like spume and there was nothing else at all in that high world and they moved all of them in a resonance that was like a music among them and they were none of them afraid horse nor colt nor

parataxis

Clauses one after another with coordinating conjunctions; clauses might occur in a long list.

A wagon train heads west in this illustration entitled *The March of Destiny*. In his novels, McCarthy rejects the romanticized view of westward expansion and the American frontier.

mare and they ran in that resonance which is the world itself and which cannot be spoken but only praised.[9]

McCarthy's poetic sense is at its peak in this mellifluous dream. John Grady is running along with the wild horses through endless fields of wildflowers, and the boy is transformed into a horse, with all the power, speed, and magic that goes with them. He and the horses moved in a resonance, and the narrator's description exceeds the dream by noting that the resonance "is the world itself" and is ineffable. (One can sense the gnostic mysticism in this claim that the world cannot be explained in words.) The fact that this is all a single long, imagistic sentence reinforces the motion of the dream and its cinematic quality. The sentence is like a film strip speeding by, projecting pictures in the air. (The first moving picture was of a running horse.)

The Country

Because *All the Pretty Horses* is what Barkley Owens calls "a retelling of the American myth of progress," it necessarily is connected to land and the idea of country.[10] The myth of the Western, which is always thought of in geographic terms, is bound up with the American dream of a better future. Owens writes,

> Americans have consistently perpetuated two frontier myths, one that champions progress and Anglo-American might and one that champions the preservation of wilderness and its idealized natives. The new world was thus viewed as two very different places: a hostile desert place full of the barbarous enemy or a pastoral Edenic garden full of idyllic innocents. Both of these ideological antipodes drew Europeans west.[11]

La Purísima represents the Garden of Eden, the biblical paradise from which Adam and Eve are expelled after their loss of innocence. John Grady and Alejandra suffer a similar fate when they refuse to follow the orders of Alejandra's family.

All the Pretty Horses presents a tension between these two images of the American frontier. Mexico in the novel is very clearly symbolic of the underworld, of a dark and lawless place full of primitive or ruthless (or both) people, dangerous weather, and a kind of animal law of survival. But why Mexico? Mexico is not west, but south. We have to remember the setting of the stories in the Border Trilogy: They take place in the early to mid-twentieth century, after the West has been settled, when "the Western frontier is gone, declared closed, moved north to Alaska or overseas to Asia. American law and government hold sway over all United States soil. To find frontier adventures, McCarthy's cowboys have only one choice."[12] They turn left, they go down, across the geographical border that symbolizes the transition that they are questing after in their own young lives. The violence and love they find in that dark underworld are the elements of their own progress.

> **archetypical**
>
> A recurring theme, setting, image, or character that seems to represent some part of a universal human nature.

The Garden of Eden

On the other hand, John Grady and Rawlins discover paradise at *La Purísima,* which literally translates to "the pure." It is the "pastoral Edenic garden full of idyllic innocents" to which Owens was referring. This special land is a symbol for the Garden of Eden, the perfect world that God creates for Adam and Eve in the first chapters of the Book of Genesis. In that archetypical story, Adam and Eve disobey God's commandment not to eat from the tree of the knowledge of good and evil; in other words, they are commanded to remain innocent and childlike. As punishment for their disobedience, God

THE "WESTERN" AS AN AMERICAN MYTHOLOGY

The Western is a literary and cinematic genre that depicts the American West during the era of American expansion, generally in the nineteenth century. Stories are told of white American settlers traveling west in wagons, braving the harsh environments, and defending themselves against outlaws or marauding Indians. Gunslingers became folk heroes. The reality was a far different story, particularly when it came to the Native Americans in the paths of the settlers.

The mythology that was forged in these types of stories was meant to explain why American is so great. According to the myths depicted in Western films and fiction, white settlers were destined to live in the West, modern civilization was destined to overtake the Indians' "primitive" culture, and as exciting as law breaking might be, it will ultimately be dealt with by the forces of order and justice.

John Wayne is probably America's most famous Western film star, portraying a rugged, supermacho gunslinger and cowboy in numerous Hollywood productions during his career (He was the lead in 142 films!). Clint Eastwood also starred in a number of Westerns and became famous as an American gunslinger, both in the Wild West and as detective Dirty Harry. While the Western reached its peak as a film genre in the 1940s to the 1960s, many interesting and successful Western films and novels have appeared since then. Clint Eastwood reprised his role as an aging alcoholic gunslinger in *Unforgiven* in 1992, which won several Academy Awards, including Best Picture and Best Director (for Eastwood himself). Other fascinating contemporary Westerns include *True Grit* (2010, a remake of a John Wayne film from 1969), *Django Unchained* (2012), and *The Assassination of Jesse James by the Coward Robert Ford* (2007).

expels Adam and Eve from the Garden to a life of hardship and pain ending in death. The Old Testament story speaks to the mortality of human beings as well as to the pain that comes with adult knowledge of the world.

John Grady and Alejandra are portrayed as Adam and Eve figures. They disobey the god-like commandments of social propriety imposed on them by Don Hector and Dueña Alfonsa, and they're expelled from *La Purísima* as a result. Grady's experience in prison is a symbolic judgment from God, and he is finally denied a return to the garden. He returns home to Texas, but not to be neatly reintegrated. He is set to wander, just as Adam must wander the dusty earth after Eden. When Grady returns Rawlins's horse back in Texas, they share a typically terse, minimalistic farewell:

> [John Grady:] I think I'm goin to move on.
>
> This is still good country.
>
> Yeah. I know it is. But it aint my country . . .
>
> Where is your country? he said.
>
> I dont know, said John Grady. I dont know where it is. I dont know what happens to country.[13]

It seems that the lesson, learned through the land itself and reflected in the loss of Eden symbolized in the story, is that adulthood undercuts simple, childish belonging to a place. The hero endlessly wanders, whether he appears in the Old Testament, in the Homeric Greek legends, in the tales of Herman Melville or Mark Twain, or in the myth of the Western in which *All the Pretty Horses* participates.

Landscape Description

Stylistically, landscape description is a crucial tool for McCarthy to evoke both familiar reality—he is said never to write about a landscape that he has not visited and explored for himself—as well as a sense of strangeness. The following passage illustrates this perfectly. It comes from late in the novel, when John Grady is traveling alone through Mexico on his return route to Texas.

> Once outside the town he left the road altogether and set off across the immense and ancient *lakebed* of the *bolsón.* He crossed a dry gypsum *playa* where the salt crust *stove* under the horse's hooves like trodden *isinglass* and he rode up through white gypsum hills grown with stunted *datil* and through a pale *bajada* crowded with flowers of *gypsum* like a *cavefloor* uncovered to the light. In the shimmering distance trees and *jacales* stood along the slender *bights* of *greenland* pale and *serried* and half *fugitive* in the clear morning air (emphasis added).[14]

The three sentences here serve to situate John Grady and his travels, but they also function like a poem, the words speaking to each other, weaving a tapestry of imagery and suggestion. For example, going off-road, John Grady rides through a lakebed, not full of water, but full of salt. It is the place where water used to be, and its ancient quality gives it the feeling of loneliness and death, of history that can't be remembered or wasn't recorded, and of a cycle

imagery

The use of visual metaphors and figurative language to create meaning or depth.

simile

Relating two unlike things using "as" or "like"; for example, "The man was as strong as a lion."

of death that haunts all of life. Isinglass has several meanings, but in the context of the American West it refers to a substance called mica, which is a glittery mineral that was used to make thin, cloudy, glasslike sheets to cover lanterns and windows, but was also in use since the paleolithic eras in North America as the powdery basis for cave paintings. We can be sure that McCarthy, when he uses a word like *isinglass*, does so with full knowledge of its typical uses and its ancient reverberations. Isinglass connects ancient people with modern America.

The pattern of flowers "like a cavefloor uncovered to the light" can be read as a straightforward simile, but it could also help bolster the coming-of-age narrative: John Grady is emerging from the darkness of his youth into the light of experience and knowledge. And this is just the moment in the novel when that is happening. The notion that the trees and jacales, which are crude, thatched huts, are "half fugitive" fits well with John Grady's state at the moment as well. He is an escaped prisoner from the corrupt Mexican penitentiary system, and he is escaping the violence of his journey, as well as the pain of the experiences he has endured.

The Crossing

The theme of borders, boundaries, and transitions is taken up with a fantastic intensity in the second novel of the trilogy, *The Crossing*, which was published in 1994. It tells the epic story of Billy Parham and his three journeys to Mexico and back. There are a number of similarities to *All the Pretty Horses*. The trajectory of the protagonists to Mexico and back is parallel. Both John Grady Cole and Billy Parham develop deep connections to the land and animals they wander among; in John Grady's case, it is the horse that he identifies with. Billy discovers a mysterious communion with a mother wolf. And

In his depiction of the hunting wolf in *The Crossing*, McCarthy conveys the beauty of violence, a prevalent theme in many of his works.

both young men are left with the scars of their experiences at the end.

The differences between the novels are perhaps more revealing, however. For instance, Billy makes three separate trips to Mexico, each revealing different truths or mysteries. The three journeys of *The Crossing* mean that this novel is more complex than its predecessor, and longer. It is philosophically deeper, and the narration is at times built layer upon layer, to an almost astonishing depth. The tone of *The Crossing* is darker and much more in line with Cormac McCarthy's signature nihilism than was *All the Pretty Horses*, which had a number of straightforward romantic elements, as we have discussed previously. Where John Grady is nominally successful—he does, in fact, meet the girl, and he walks out of Mexico one horse richer—Billy Parham is utterly destitute at the end of *The Crossing*, having lost his parents, the wolf, and finally his younger brother Boyd.

"At Once Terrible and of a Great Beauty": The Wolf

From John Grady's dreams of running with wild horses, the running animal returns in *The Crossing* as a wolf, to symbolize a natural, ancient, and mysterious energy that connects everything in the universe. At the beginning of the novel, a young Billy witnesses a pack of wolves hunting a pack of antelope in the very early morning. The hunters and hunted are figured like dancers in a silent ballet. "The antelope moved like phantoms in the snow and circled and wheeled" while they seemed to burn "with some inner fire," and the "wolves twisted and turned and leapt in a silence such that they seemed of another world entire."[15] Already in the first pages of the novel, Billy is the human witness to the other-worldly animal energy of violence, a violence that he will have to come to terms with

A nineteenth-century painting depicts Sodom and Gomorrah, two biblical cities destroyed by God because of their sinfulness. In *Cities of the Plain,* El Paso and Juarez serve as modern-day counterparts of the corrupt ancient cities.

over the course of his life. By the end of part one, which is primarily concerned with his first crossing to Mexico, ostensibly to save the she-wolf he's captured near the family ranch, he has begun to discover the place he occupies in this cosmic flow. The wolf has been stolen from him and forced to fight in brutal dogfights to the death. Billy breaks her free, but she is already mortally wounded, so he takes her to the hills to bury her. The scene bookends his earlier vision of the wolves on their hunt.

Billy "put his hand upon her bloodied forehead and closed his own eyes that he could see her running in the mountains, running in the starlight where the grass was wet," reunited with those earlier wolves, free to run. But the running of the wolves was never something he could harness; the wild was never anything that humans could dominate. Billy lifted "her stiff head out of the leaves and held it or he reached to hold what cannot be held, what already ran among the mountains at once terrible and of a great beauty."[16] The wolf is a symbol of the terrible beauty that Billy recognizes is uncontainable and not something that he needs to or could save, even if wanted to. The rest of the novel will be an account of Billy trying to reckon, to use one of McCarthy's favorite words, with what is essentially "beyond reckoning." In other words, these stories will not leave us any closer to understanding the world or their own lives, except insofar as they help us recognize a strange and potentially dangerous meaninglessness that threads through existence. This is the nihilism—the belief in nothingness—that pervades McCarthy's work (see Chapter 2).

Cities of the Plain

The conclusion to the Border Trilogy centers on the twin cities of El Paso, Texas, and Juárez, Mexico. They sit on opposite sides of the United States–Mexico border, and the friction that occurs at that point of contact can produce intense heat. The phrase that makes up the title of the novel, "cities of the plain," is a reference to the story of Sodom and Gomorrah, told in the book of Genesis. In Chapter 18 of that book, Sodom and Gomorrah were said to be two cities in which every person had been corrupted by sin. God sent messengers to save his disciple named Lot, as well as Lot's family, but then leveled the rest, killing everyone else. It is the quintessential example of divine justice, and the story has come to be an emblem of corruption and sexual deviance (which is what the citizens of the cities of the plains were accused of by God).

This biblical frame fits the novel, since El Paso and Juárez are both corrupted by corporate interests, crime, prostitution, and, significantly, drugs. John Grady Cole and Billy Parham are both working for the same ranch. John Grady falls in love with a prostitute from Juárez and plans to settle down with her. Her pimp kills her (horribly, of course), and John Grady fights him to the death, killing the pimp but also receiving a mortal wound. Billy survives to find a new community—much like the survival of Lot in the biblical account—but not before meeting an old man under a bridge who, it is implied, is Death himself.

The Old Gives Way to the New

What is ultimately important about the Border Trilogy, and perhaps of McCarthy's novels in general, is the idea that the old ways are constantly being destroyed and replaced by new ways. This is a vague way of saying that history or historical progress is a violent, ugly process. We like to think of progress as something really good, something desirable. We imagine new technology or new medicine. But McCarthy's stories will always be there to remind us that what we have now is the result of a long series of terrible and bloody encounters—from the old ways of Mexico being overturned in the Mexican Revolution, to the Wild West being paved over and mapped, to the post–World War II era of guns, drugs, and crime—traditions and forms of life will always be crushed under the pressure of what is insistently new.

How It All Ends: *The Road* and the End of History

W hen we think about Cormac McCarthy's work in general, we have to realize that most of it centers on destruction, devastation, violence, and in the case of *The Road*, the end of the entire world. End-of-the-world tales are also known as apocalypse stories. A story about the apocalypse can have different features: it can be about a local disaster, such as a deadly hurricane that wipes out a city (but not the entire planet); on the other hand, it could feature a planet-ending catastrophe, like a giant comet hitting Earth, causing a mass extinction. So apocalypses can be local or global. They can also be comic or tragic, and here we use an old distinction between stories with happy endings, where people continue living in happy communities, and stories with sad endings, where everyone dies alone. (It's pretty much that simple!)

The other major differences among apocalypse stories are about *why* the catastrophe takes place. Is it a natural disaster, like in the film *The Day After Tomorrow*? A plague, like in *28 Days Later*? An invading army, like the book *All Quiet on the Western Front*? Or an invading army of aliens, as in *The War of the Worlds*? Is there some supernatural element, like the film *Ghostbusters*? Or is the catastrophe unwittingly triggered by humans, like the invention of an artificial intelligence that

A fifteenth-century illustration of the Four Horsemen of the Apocalypse: Conquest, War, Famine, and Death.

ends up coming back to control us? (The *Terminator* series picks up this plotline, and even includes elements of time travel.) Many apocalypse stories mix and match these features to create new and entertaining spectacles of disaster.

Deciding what kind of apocalypse we're reading can help us determine the best way to analyze it. If we already know the basic shape of the drama, then we can see where it doesn't quite fit the genre. The moments when a text veers away from convention are often the most interesting, and the most worth writing about. After learning about the story and its characters, we will return to the question: What kind of apocalypse is *The Road*? Keep that question at the back of your mind, because the answer is unusual and makes this novel well worth our attention.

Publication History

The Road was published in 2006 and won the 2007 Pulitzer Prize for fiction. In 2009 it was adapted to film. It is a departure for McCarthy since it moves his well-worn setting east toward the Atlantic coast, but it also represents his first science fiction novel. The story is very simple: A man and his son ("the boy") are traveling together through a wasteland that is evidently the result of some kind of incendiary apocalypse. We don't know what exactly happened, but it was terrible and relatively quick. The man and the boy have to avoid roving bands of men and women who are intent on finding people, imprisoning them, and eating them bit by bit. Because the world has been burned, there isn't any plant life to speak of, no wild game or fish. Human flesh, therefore, becomes a valuable calorie source. The man has a pistol, but he only has two bullets, and he saves them for the boy and himself, should they be surrounded or cornered by cannibals. The man is sick—with what seems like

Cormac McCarthy attends the 2009 premiere of *The Road* in New York City. While he did visit the set during filming, McCarthy was not involved in the production of the movie.

a respiratory disease—and near the end of the novel he dies. The boy meets a new family, who offer to take him in, and the book ends on an uncharacteristically hopeful note.

"Carrying the Fire"

One of the central themes, repeated throughout the text, is the idea of "carrying the fire." The boy asks his father:

> We're going to be okay, arent we Papa?
>
> Yes. We are.
>
> And nothing bad is going to happen to us.
>
> That's right.
>
> Because we're carrying the fire.
>
> Yes. Because we're carrying the fire.[1]

The fire they carry is a moral light, the metaphor they have chosen to indicate that they are different from the "bad guys" who eat other people. The moral fire contrasts with the actual fires that they struggle to build each night. In the end, as his father lies dying near the beach, the boy begs his father to stay, and then begs to go with him. The man refuses to kill his son and insists that the boy go on carrying the fire. When the boy meets a stranger on the beach who claims to be part of a family, the boy asks:

> How do I know you're one of the good guys?
>
> You dont. You'll have to take a shot.
>
> Are you carrying the fire?

Am I what?

Carrying the fire.

You're kind of weirded out, arent you?

No.

Just a little.

Yeah.

That's okay.

So are you?

What, carrying the fire?

Yes.

Yeah. We are.[2]

The stranger seems to intuit what the boy is referring to, and this is a signal that he is in fact "carrying the fire." He knows what it means without needing an explanation. The fire, then, is what makes the last scenes of the novel, which are heartbreaking, ultimately a hopeful conclusion.

"They Went On": An American Road Trip

Obviously *The Road* is the story of a journey, and McCarthy's choice of style for this novel helps us understand what kind of journey this might be, and what kinds of interpretations we might unravel from it. Unlike the other great journeys in McCarthy's body of work, in particular the Mexican novels, *The Road* maintains elements of hopefulness and redemption throughout, despite the horrors the man and the boy encounter. This contrast between what seems like a terrible, destroyed world and the moral or spiritual possibilities of the future is played out in the contrast between McCarthy's archaic, apocalyptic language—the kind of language you'd read in *Blood Meridian*, say—and the stark, minimalist prose of the journey itself. For example, more than thirty times in the text McCarthy writes, "they went on." The bleak simplicity of this phrase might suggest that they merely moved forward, without purpose, and that the future held little except what they had already encountered. But the movement through the world isn't simple, as we can read in an early episode where the man and the boy are traveling through an urban landscape.

> By dusk of the day following they were at the city. The long concrete sweeps of the interstate exchanges like the ruins of a vast funhouse against the distant murk. He carried the revolver in his belt at the front and wore his parka unzipped. The mummied dead everywhere. The flesh cloven along the bones, the ligaments dried to tug and taut as wires. Shriveled and drawn like latterday bogfolk, their faces of boiled sheeting, the yellowed palings of their teeth. They were discalced to a man like pilgrims of some common order for all their shoes were long since stolen. They went on.[3]

This grotesque imagery—of the ruins of a funhouse, the murk, the mummified dead, the rotten and dried flesh—builds up around the travelers, and the descriptions are precise. But the travelers don't react. Instead of stopping to make sense of the death around them, "they went on" through the gloom. The travelers are the future and have to leave this scene behind them. The "discalced" population of the city represent the failed religious orders of the past, religion that, it is hinted, might have caused the world to burn in the first place (although this is never made explicit).

The Imagination of Disaster

In 1965, a famous literary and cultural critic named Susan Sontag wrote a short essay with the title "The Imagination of Disaster." In it, Sontag explores the meaning of science fiction films, a genre of entertainment that was carving out a permanent space in the American cultural landscape. Sontag's central argument is that science fiction stories of the twentieth century (and, let us extrapolate, into the twenty-first century) are fueled by an "imagination of disaster" that appears to be particularly interested in the aesthetics of destruction, moral simplification, a technological view of violence, and the playing out of various personal and political fantasies.[4] The disaster narrative, for Sontag, allows the audience to watch the spectacle of destruction and, through that awful violence, express a cathartic need for retaliation or salvation. In other words, we love watching explosions, for example, because they are resolved on the screen, not in real life.

The disaster narrative also reflects the need for modern culture to make sense of traumatic situations, such as the aftermath of World War II or the possibility of nuclear annihilation. Sontag is worried, though, that we are not reacting as strongly to the possible apocalypse as we need to in order to take it seriously. In the end, "The Imagination of Disaster" is an attempt to remind us that art has a very real function in society, far beyond being a simple diversion from the drudgery of everyday life. Similar calls can be heard from politicians, scientists, and activists on the subject of climate change: watching a film about climate change may actually make you

A scene from *Mad Max: Fury Road*, a post-apocalyptic film released in 2015. Critic Susan Sontag believes that seeing disaster and destruction on a movie screen desensitizes us to the real possibility of the end of the world.

more likely to *ignore* the issue in real life, since the problem has been solved on screen.

A number of critics of *The Road* have noted that it depicts what could easily be a post-climate change world, and as such it falls under the rubric of science fiction (as Sontag discusses it) or speculative fiction (à la Margaret Atwood). How does Cormac McCarthy represent this apocalypse? And is he using the techniques of the "spectacle" that Sontag warns us about?

In contrast to the splashy Hollywood alien invasion or viral apocalypses of the past fifty years, *The Road* is simple, minimal, almost not there. Instead of the "aesthetics of destruction" of massive explosions that Sontag writes about, McCarthy highlights the poetry of starvation, the painful beauty of loss, and the awful silence that accompanies the aftermath of destruction. The landscape is dead, depleted. "The land was gullied and eroded and barren. The bones of dead creatures sprawled in the washes. Middens of anonymous trash. Farmhouses in the field scoured of their paint and the clapboards spooned and sprung from the wall-studs. All of it shadowless and without feature."[5] Barrenness and emptiness is the spectacle that McCarthy offers in place of the fires of anni-hilation. The fact that the landscape is shadowless deepens the imagery rather than reduces it; the sun is not shining directly on houses and bones and gullies, and so we do not reap what potentially uplifting benefit there is in the bright light of day.

Sontag understands the appeal of sci-fi/horror films to be, in part, based on the "undeniable pleasure we derive from looking at freaks" because they allows us to engage "a morally acceptable fantasy" in which "the sense of superiority over the freak" combined with "the titillation of fear and aversion makes it possible for moral scruples to be lifted, for cruelty to be enjoyed."[6] (Flannery O'Connor would disagree with this

In *The Road*, the initial disaster is not important, and is only briefly described. For McCarthy, the interest lies in what is left and how people act in the post-apocalyptic setting.

argument; see Chapter 2). *The Road* capitalizes on superiority over freaks, "the freakish, the ugly and the predatory."[7] In *The Road* the world is divided into good guys and bad guys, the kind of simplification that one finds in comic books and Westerns, or the political rhetoric of contemporary American foreign policy. The story emphasizes "carrying the fire," remaining virtuous and decent in the face of ugliness. When we read this book, we might indulge the fantasy that "we would act that way, too."

But for the man in the novel, the simplification of good and bad is both an acknowledgment of the truth of their situation and a necessary irony that helps him make sense of the world for his son. The good guys "carry the fire,"

> **irony**
>
> When meaning is different from use, or when what comes to pass is not typical or expected.

the bad guys murder and eat people. The man and the boy are not on a crusade to annihilate the bad guys, as would be the case in a typical Western; they just want to avoid them and survive. The bad guys in *The Road* function like the zombies in a horror film: freaks to be feared, avoided at all costs, killed when necessary, pitied when possible. By simplifying morality into good and bad, the novel seems to follow certain genre conventions of Westerns, science fiction, and horror, but the simplification is always partly ironic. No one is entirely good or entirely bad, as the father shows in his angry cruelty toward anyone who might threaten them.

What Caused the Apocalypse?

McCarthy refrains from spelling out the precise details of his imagined future, which allows him to suggest multiple possibilities and to play with multiple ironies. The novel implies that

THE ROAD AND THE WALKING DEAD

Is *The Road* a zombie novel? It's possible. Since the mega-popularity of zombie fiction, film, and television in the past ten years, it's a relevant question. Consider AMC's hit TV series *The Walking Dead* (based on a graphic novel series of the same title). Like *The Road*, it centers much of the narrative on a father-son duo coming to grips with a frightening post-apocalyptic landscape. Like *The Road*, there are roving mobs of people bent on either killing or eating them. And like *The Road*, the main characters are fighting not just for survival, but to maintain some semblance of righteous or moral life.

There are several moments in *The Road* that point explicitly to zombies. Of course, there are the scenes of outright cannibalism. Beyond these, however, the boy's mother wonders if they aren't actually "walking dead in a horror film."[8] In another scene, the man wakes during the night:

> At night when he woke coughing he'd sit up with his hand pushed over his head against the blackness. Like a man waking in a grave. Like those disinterred dead from his childhood that had been relocated to accommodate a highway. Many had died in a cholera epidemic and they'd been buried in haste in wooden boxes and the boxes were rotting and falling open. The dead came to light lying on their sides with their legs drawn up and some lay on their stomachs. The dull green antique coppers spilled from out the tills of their eyesockets onto the stained and rotted coffin floors.[9]

Here the man is becoming a zombie as his life drains away, and McCarthy gives us clear images of dead bodies rising from the ground, to make the connection even stronger.

religious fanatics caused *The Road*'s incendiary apocalypse, fulfilling their own prophecies of doom. Religion, instead of being a source of salvation, is ironically made into the very source of destruction. The ultimate American action hero is a lone gunman facing down the evil hordes arrayed against him. McCarthy's hero, though, is in pitiful condition and ultimately dies. He does not face the hordes, he avoids them.

The man's gun, a symbol of heroism in the American West, contains only two, then finally a single, bullet, which he reserves so that he might kill his child in the event that they are captured or cornered. In a sinister but very realistic move, the gun that fuels the American myth of heroic individualism in the Wild West is turned on the hero in a suicidal gesture. (Death is the only protection against the world.) Finally, the irony that the world has burned plays with the contemporary communal understanding of the dangers of global warming: Consumerism ends up consuming everything, even itself. But none of these ironies land as wry comedy; they come across matter-of-factly, pitifully plain, and sad. They are all equally likely, both in the novel and in the world around us: the violence of religious fanaticism, the myth of the gun slinger, and the disaster of global warming.

Time and No Time: A Future With No Future

The Road operates on several temporal levels simultaneously: calendar time, story time, and the absence of time (or, the end of time). The main plot takes place over the course of what seems to be a couple of months: this is calendar time. Under normal circumstances, that would be sufficient to render time physically. The seasons might change, color might appear in the surrounding plants and trees, birds might return after a long winter, and so on. But the setting of *The Road* forecloses this possibility. Earth has been burned to a gray char, all the trees are burned up and dead, and there aren't any more birds. There is no color and thus no time. (What an intriguing connection between color and time!)

We are reminded of this in the first few lines of the text, which present a world of "nights dark beyond darkness and the days more gray each one than what had gone before. Like the onset of some cold glaucoma dimming away the world . . ."[10] Even the sun, whose daily trek across the sky might signal the passage of time, is blocked by the clouds of ash and smog kicked up by the burning world: the "banished sun circles the earth like a grieving mother with a lamp." [11] There are no stars, there is no moon. The heavens, where Chronos (the ancient Greek god of time; hence the word *chronological*) himself originated, have been erased.

Early in the text, the man wakes before the boy and he "studied the country to the south. Barren, silent, godless. He thought the month was October but he wasnt sure. He hadnt kept a calendar for years."[12] Starvation—the shrinking of their bodies—is the only sustained change left to mark the passage of time. This is what you might call story time or, time as it is expressed through narrative elements. The world and their bodies wasting slowly away: Whatever danger they face from other travelers on the road, this inexorable process is the only form of change, leading to death, "the final form of change."[13] The world is dimming away, and language itself is fading:

> He tried to think of something to say and could not ... The world shrinking down about a raw core of parsible entities. The names of things slowly following those things into oblivion. Colors. The names of birds. Things to eat. Finally the names of things one believed to be

true ... Drawing down like something trying to preserve heat. In time to wink out forever.[14]

McCarthy's metaphors are consistent. The world is a slowly dying fire, or a cooling piece of charcoal, already burned and dead, now simply consuming itself. The self-consumption of a piece of charcoal aligns neatly with the cannibalism that the man and the boy witness throughout the story. The cannibals signal that this is a population feeding on itself until it "winks out forever."

The winking out of the light is the dissolution of the world, of life, the end of history. "The frailty of everything revealed at last. Old and troubling issues resolved into nothingness and night. The last instance of a thing takes the class with it. Turns out the light and is gone. Look around you. Ever is a long time. But the boy knew what he knew. That ever is no time at all."[15] Ever, or forever, is reduced to a pinpoint, a temporal singularity, the mere breath of a moment. It is the opposite of the eternity of Heaven. Hell in *The Road* is defined by fire (the world has burned up), but it is also devoid of warmth. It's a place with no geography (the map they follow is in tattered pieces), a story with no time, and a life that is really just a kind of "walking death," as the boy's mother rightly points out before she commits suicide.

> **in media res**
>
> Latin phrase that means "into the middle of things"; used to describe a story that begins in the middle of the action, rather than at the beginning of a chronological tale.

The plot doesn't even seem to have a recognizable story time by providing a solid beginning and a punchy end. We join the action *in media res*, in the midst of a survival journey already a decade old (given the approximate age of the boy),

In the film adaptation of *The Road*, Viggo Mortensen and Kodi Smit-McPhee play the roles of the man and the boy. McCarthy based that relationship on his own relationship with his son John.

and the story ends (also approximately) with the father's death, the boy speaking to the father in prayer. The man's death, while biographically significant, is softened by the boy continuing to speak to him, as if the ghost of his father is still present. The man's death is not a satisfaction or resolution of anything.

Intensity of the Present

This, then, is the nature of time in *The Road*: a ghostly time, nailed to the present, in which the two heroes are totally devoted to one another. All events seem to take place outside realistic time, in a demonic dreamscape, yet paradoxically each episode in the journey exists in the hyperrealism and suspense of the present moment. McCarthy sometimes uses the intricacies of survivalist techniques to evoke this realism, as the man scavenges parts from stoves or rigs up some pathetic shelter that will only just save their two lives from the ravages of exposure. Taking what he can from a wrecked sailboat off the coast, the man

> ...went back into the galley and opened the toolbox and set about removing one of the burners from the little gimballed stove. He disconnected the braided flexline and removed the aluminum spiders from the burners and put one of them in the pocket of his coat. He unfastened the brass fittings with a wrench and took the burners loose. Then he uncoupled them and fastened the hose to the coupling pipe and fitted the other end of the hose to the gasbottle and carried it out to the saloon.[16]

The detailed account of actions—mechanical and chronological—are in stark contrast to the nightmarish existence out on the road. Each phrase and sentence keeps the narration in a sequential present, and the specificity of the man's actions make us trust in its reality. This procedural reporting is reminiscent of Hemingway's Santiago in *The Old Man and the Sea* gathering his gear before his fateful expedition, or Nick's expert fly-fishing techniques at the end of Hemingway's collection of short stories, *In Our Time*. But the resemblance can only be ironic: the man in the *The Road* is pitting his wits and spirit not against the vitality of Nature, but against the black hole of a dead Earth.

Time, throughout the novel, is condensed to a highly intense, almost visceral sense of the present. The boy wakes from sleep: "Can I ask you something? he said. / Yes. Of course. / Are we going to die? / Sometime. Not now."[17] Death is inevitable. What matters is what will happen now. The man and the boy are not changed by events: if there is change then there is a sense of history, and here there is none of that. The man and the boy are bonded by an ever-present and eternal (one might call it unconditional) love, which, for the man at least, borders on the transcendent or religious. "He knew only that the child was his warrant. He said: If he is not the word of God God never spoke."[18] We learn about his fervent devotion to the boy from the very first pages, and this devotion, being total, never grows, and it certainly never diminishes. As Mikhail Bakhtin explains when describing the kind of time that operates in adventure-time, "the love between the hero and heroine is not subject to doubt; this love remains absolutely unchanged throughout the entire novel."[19] The father-son pairing here isn't romantic, but love has the same effect in *The Road*. Their love is absolute and unchanging.

In many adventure novels there are significant biographical events that provide a kind of map for the story: birth, marriage, death, etc. In this novel, there are two biographically significant moments: the birth of the boy, which we access through the man's memory, and the death of the man, which we access through the boy's experience. And yet nothing is consummated or satisfied in *The Road*. The man's death is not an ending, just as the boy's birth is not a beginning. What fire is "winking out" in the world is not extinguished in the boy: he carries it forward at the end. In order to fully appreciate this novel, we should be aware of the complex relationship it has to time: calendar time, story time, the chronology of events, and so on. Put simply, *The Road* is operating on three levels of temporality. First, the man and the boy are suspended in a kind of unmoving, singular time: *Now*. Second, because of the fact that it's a story about the end of the world, the novel is speaking to the future: *Soon*. And finally, because the form it takes is an ancient journey narrative, it is also speaking to the distant past: *Back then*.

The Connections Between Future Catastrophe and Ancient Myths: Biblical Language and Allusion

In what other ways is this novel connected to an ancient or mythological past? Robert Alter's analysis of *The Road* as a text steeped in Biblical material and style can help us understand how the novel simultaneously reaches back to an epic past and to the particular history of America. In his book *Pen of Iron*, Alter makes the case that American literature has been, since its inauguration, heavily influenced by the King James Version of the Bible (KJB) in ways that are unique to that nation. The United States is, according to Alter, a nation of the Bible, or a "scriptural culture."[20] This is not to say that Americans are all necessarily religious, but that from the Pilgrims onward, the Old Testament has played a vital role in American literature and culture.

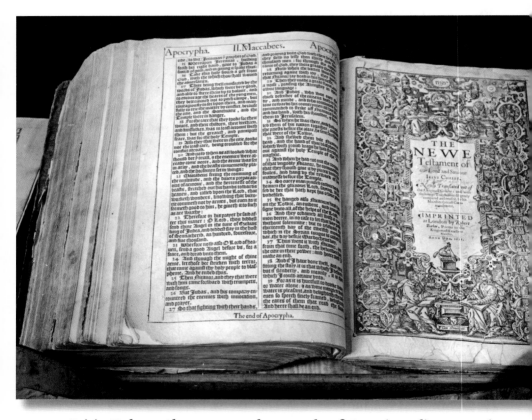

Critic Robert Alter argues that much of American literature is influenced by the King James Version of the Bible. Specifically, *The Road* melds the style of the Old Testament with the focus on the future that is found in the New Testament.

Alter argues that the Old Testament held more sway than the New Testament because "the anchorage of Hebrew Scripture in ideas of family, nationhood, land and politics spoke to the early settlers . . . in ways that the New Testament could not . . .".[21] This was because the Old Testament "was pervaded by a sense of national destiny deeply engaged in history" whereas the New Testament "addressed individuals in urgent need of salvation as the kingdom—which is to say, the end of history—was about to come."[22] That is, the Old Testament speaks to history, the New Testament to the end of the world. In any case, since the Biblical style is so evident in so much of American culture and literature, we must bear in mind that "style is not merely a constellation of aesthetic properties but is the vehicle of a particular vision of reality."[23] The King James Version, therefore, can be read as "the vehicle for certain distinctively American constructions of reality."[24]

The Old Testament, Alter reminds us, relates to the foundation of a nation, which is rooted in family, country, and land. America under the sway of the Hebrew Scriptures was, Alter says, "pervaded by a sense of national destiny." It is clear that the history of America really has been driven by a sense of destiny, even to the point of calling itself "Manifest Destiny" and justifying the horrors of Westward Expansion. (This is one of the ways of understanding *Blood Meridian*.) The New Testament, on the other hand, looks forward to the end of history. *The Road*, it seems, can be situated as a bridge between these two competing and complementary attitudes to time. On the one hand, *The Road* is steeped in the linguistic style of the Old Testament, as Alter shows, and it even contains some direct allusions. On the other hand, the novel is set in the future, and it emerges from a modern American perspective toward an imminent end of history, as the New Testament stresses, involving both religious fanaticism and environmental destruction. *The Road* is a combination of Old and New Testament elements in a single text.

Parataxis

Alter locates the connection between *The Road* and the KJB in McCarthy's parataxis, which is the technique of connecting lists of subordinate clauses, descriptions, or sentences with little more than simple punctuation or the conjunction *and*. This technique, he argues, is typical of the KJB, and it helps to make the KJB sound a certain way. McCarthy picks up on the sound of the Bible and integrates it into his storytelling. The effect of this is to make the boy seem more than a boy. He seems like a version of Jesus, a holy son, and the father is like a kind of God. (In the final pages, the boy is encouraged to pray to God, but he can only pray to his dead father.)

Cannibalism

Aside from Alter's association of McCarthy's style and Biblical mythology, *The Road*'s repeated concern with killing or eating one's own children evokes mythological and Biblical motifs. When the man and the boy encounter a headless newborn, charred, hanging on a spit over a campfire, they turn away in despair. But McCarthy has given us that image, as haunting as Goya's "Saturn Devouring His Son," which melds the gruesome parent–child violence of Greek and Roman mythology with the violence at the core of human existence. The scene from *The Road* with the baby on a spit, one of the most horrible in the novel, is left out of the film version. In place of it, the man and the boy watch as a young boy and his mother are overtaken by a gang of men, struck down in the road. The film leaves out the explicit practice of breeding people for food. Perhaps in this case the immediacy that Sontag thinks is the peculiar power of film is too much: it is too much to watch it, but reading about it might just be possible, and in that way we can confront these horrible scenes of carnage.

Examples of parents eating their own children in Greek mythology are too common to be ignored: Tantalus, Atreus and Thyestes, Zeus, and Father Time himself, Chronos. But the horror of killing one's own son (other than to eat them) is also a powerful mythological concern. Medea is the most well-known child-killing character of Greek tragedy, but Abraham (who, in the biblical book of Genesis is commanded by God to sacrifice his only son on an altar), as well as the Christian myth of the death of Jesus, are perhaps the stronger claims to meaning here. Given McCarthy's characterization of the boy as "messianic,"[25] the man's struggle to commit to killing the boy out of mercy resonates with God's lament at the death of his "only begotten son." Through the sacrifice of a father for his son, and of the son for his father, one could read the whole novel as a nonspiritual account of the story of Christ.

Religious Fanaticism

America as a fanatically Christian nation: Is this what the ghastly imagery of cannibalism and immolation suggest? For instance, an interlude to the action of the novel provides some cloaked insight into the global apocalypse's cause:

> People sitting on the sidewalk in the dawn half immolate and smoking in their clothes. Like failed sectarian suicides. Others would come to help them. Within a year there were fires on the ridges and deranged chanting. The screams of the murdered. By day the dead impaled on spikes along the road. What had they done?[26]

McCarthy explores themes of death, religion, and good versus evil as the man and his son make their pilgrimage toward an unknown destination.

These figures have failed in their actions, and require help from others. The fanaticism is just getting started. But what is happening here? The fires on the ridges, deranged chanting, and the screams of the murdered all seem to portray a kind of fanatical madness and demonic ritual sacrifice. It is a fiery, extreme version of Christianity, with its dogmatic truths, fervent faiths, rituals of self-sacrifice, and ultimately, the cannibalism inherent in the Eucharist, during which participants eat the flesh and drink the blood of Christ.

The ghostly presence of religious fanaticism seems to hover over the man's memory. "On this road there are no godspoke men. They are gone and I am left and they have taken with them the world. Query: How does the never to be differ from what never was?"[27] The word *godspoke* obtrudes because it is wholly ambiguous. It could mean that there are no prophets or religious leaders—those to whom God speaks—which implies that the religious fanatics have consumed themselves and have "taken with them the world" by destroying it. It could mean, on the other hand, that what is lost is faith itself, that whoever is left on the road has abandoned belief in God; no one speaks to God anymore. Whichever it means, God is as absent as those to whom he spoke or who spoke to him, because the lack of godspoke men applies to the man as well. The final query is yet another identification between the emptiness of the apocalyptic landscape and the emptiness of the past that caused it, all presented as an emptiness of time, a series of nevers. The absence of time—never—is the moment of ultimate human tragedy. The "never to be" is essentially the same as the "never that was."

Cormac McCarthy's Originality

Most of this book has been devoted to not only understanding the works of McCarthy, but to placing those works in context and understanding how he weaves together older—at times, ancient—influences in his stories. Ultimately, however, what is striking about McCarthy's body of work is its potent originality. He has invented a style that, while it draws from other times, places, and modes of thought—ancient Greece and old Christianity, the American South and West, Faulkner and O'Connor, archaeology and botany—it remains unique to Cormac McCarthy. To illustrate this in a humorous way, we might refer to a popular blog, *Yelping With Cormac*. The author writes fake reviews, as if posting them on Yelp.com, of businesses and restaurants (e.g. the Apple store in San Francisco, or Chipotle Mexican Grill) in McCarthy's style.

Chipotle Mexican Grill

Three stars.

See that false burrito. See it swaddled in tinfoil on the desk in the bowels of that great tower, a bundle of meat and sauce in a place long ago ceded to silicone and copper. The stooped man eating that peasant food as if in consuming it he can escape to a farmfield in a verdant valley and look down and see blood running from his blisters and say, yes this is work. This is work. Instead his hands are clawlike and ruined by the keyboard and the mouse for he is a thing of bone and sinew in a sprawling contraption electric and of man's creation but not of man at all."[29]

We can recognize the nod to the opening of *Blood Meridian* ("See the child") and the intense imagery that evoke body parts, misery, and blood. But even without pointing out exactly how, the tongue-in-cheek review is unmistakably McCarthian, a kind of sober accounting of a human disaster to remind us that we are both the source of violence in everyday life and its victims. Strangely, *Yelping With Cormac* is solid proof that Cormac McCarthy has already carved a permanent place in American literature and will not soon be forgotten.

CHRONOLOGY

1933— Charles "Cormac" McCarthy is born on July 20 in Providence, Rhode Island.

1937— Moves with family to Knoxville, Tennessee.

1951— Attends the University of Tennessee for one year.

1961— Marries first wife Lee Holleman.

1962— Birth of McCarthy's first son, Cullen.

1965— McCarthy's first novel, *The Orchard Keeper*, is published and wins the William Faulkner Foundation Award.

1966— Marries second wife Anne DeLisle in England. They move to the Spanish island of Ibiza.

1967— Moves back to Tennessee with DeLisle.

1968— Publishes *Outer Dark*, his second novel, about an incestuous relationship between a brother and sister.

1973— Publishes *Child of God*, about a necrophiliac serial killer named Lester Ballard.

1976— Writes *The Gardener's Son*, a screenplay for a special two-hour episode of the TV show *Visions*. Separates from DeLisle and moves to El Paso, Texas.

1979— *Suttree* is published; the only novel of McCarthy's that is remotely autobiographical.

1981— Wins the MacArthur Fellowship (also known as the genius grant).

1985— Publishes his masterpiece, *Blood Meridian, or the Evening Redness in the West*.

1992— Releases the first of the Border Trilogy, *All the Pretty Horses*.

1994— Publishes second installment of the Border Trilogy, *The Crossing*. Continued commercial success.

1997— Receives the Texas Institute of Letters Lon Tinkle Lifetime Achievement Award.

1998— Completes the Border Trilogy cycle with *Cities of the Plain*.

2000— Film adaptation of *All the Pretty Horses* is released, directed by Billy Bob Thornton.

2001— Houston staging of his play *The Stonemason: A Play in Five Acts*, which had been published about a decade before.

2005— Charts a new direction in *No Country for Old Men*, including a contemporary setting, hit men, and a more conventional action plot.

2006— Supposedly written in a few weeks, McCarthy publishes *The Road* to blockbuster success.

2007— *The Road* wins the Pulitzer Prize for fiction. McCarthy sits for his only televised interview, with Oprah Winfrey.

2009— Film adaptation of *The Road* is released in theaters. Receives the PEN/Saul Bellow Award for lifetime achievement in American fiction.

2011— Writes a screenplay for a play he published in 2006, *The Sunset Limited*; film version stars Tommy Lee Jones and Samuel Jackson.

2013— *The Counselor* is released in theaters; first major Hollywood film based on an original screenplay by McCarthy, directed by Ridley Scott.

CHAPTER NOTES

Introduction. An Unmistakable Author

1. James Wood, "Red Planet," *The New Yorker Magazine,* July 25, 2005, www.newyorker.com/magazine/2005/07/25/red-planet.

Chapter 1. A Slow and Steady Rise to Prominence

1. Oprah Winfrey interview with Cormac McCarthy, *Oprah .com,* accessed November 18, 2015, www.oprah.com/oprahsbookclub/Oprahs-Exclusive-Interview-with-Cormac-McCarthy-Video.
2. Noah Gallagher Shannon, "Cormac McCarthy Cuts to the Bone," October 5, 2012, *Slate.com,* www.slate.com/articles/arts/books/2012/10/cormac_mccarthy_s_blood_meridian_early_drafts_and_history_.html.

Chapter 2. The Dark World of McCarthy's Fiction

1. Cormac McCarthy, *All the Pretty Horses* (New York: Vintage Books, 1993), 302.
2. Flannery O'Connor, "Some Aspects of the Grotesque in Southern Literature," in *Mystery and Manners: Occasional Prose* (New York: Farrar, Straus, & Giroux, 1970), 41–42.
3. Tim Parrish, "The Killer Wears the Halo: Cormac McCarthy, Flannery O'Connor, and the American Religion," in *Sacred Violence, Vol. 1: Cormac McCarthy's Appalachian Works* (El Paso: Texas Western Press, 2002), 37.
4. Cormac McCarthy, *Blood Meridian, or, the Evening Redness in the West* (New York: Vintage, 1992), 330.

Chapter 3. "War Is the Ultimate Game": *Blood Meridian*

1. J. Molinaro, "The Scalp Hunters," December 1, 1997, xroads. virginia.edu/~hyper/HNS/Scalpin/apaches.html.
2. John C. Cremony, *Life Among the Apaches* (New York: A. Roman & Co., 1868), 116.
3. Cremony, 117.
4. Ibid.
5. *Blood Meridian*, 323.
6. Ibid.
7. Dana Phillips, "History and the Ugly Facts of Cormac McCarthy's Blood Meridian," in *American Literature* 68, no. 2 (1968): 443.
8. Ibid.
9. Ibid.
10. *Blood Meridian*, 19.
11. Ibid., 245.
12. Ibid., 248.
13. Ibid.
14. Eccles. 1:2.
15. Eccles. 8:13.
16. Eric Miles Williamson, "Beyond Good and Evil," *The Los Angeles Times*, July 24, 2005, articles.latimes.com/2005/ jul/24/books/bk-williamson24.
17. Vince Brewton, "The Changing Landscape of Violence in Cormac McCarthy's Early Novels and the Border Trilogy," in *Southern Literary Journal* 37, no. 1 (2004): 123.
18. *Blood Meridian*, 249.
19. Ibid.
20. Ibid.
21. Ibid.

22. Ibid., 329.

23. Cormac McCarthy, *No Country For Old Men* (New York: Vintage, 2007), 56–57.

Chapter 4. The Border Trilogy

1. Gloria Anzaldúa, *Borderlands/La Frontera: The New Mestiza* (San Francisco: Aunt Lute Books, 2007), 3.

2. Margaret Atwood, *In Other Worlds: Science Fiction and the Human Imagination* (New York: Anchor, 2011), 67.

3. Ibid., 75.

4. Daniel Cooper Alarcón, "All The Pretty Mexicos: Cormac McCarthy's Mexican Representations," in *Cormac McCarthy: new directions* (Albuquerque: University of New Mexico Press, 2002), 145.

5. Alarcón, 149.

6. Gail Moore Morrison, "All the Pretty Horses: John Grady Cole's Expulsion from Paradise," in *Perspectives on Cormac McCarthy* (Jackson, MS: University Press of Mississippi, 1993), 174–175.

7. Jonathan Franzen, *Freedom* (New York: Macmillan, 2010), 318.

8. Cormac McCarthy, *All the Pretty Horses* (New York: Vintage Books, 1993), 5.

9. Ibid., 161.

10. Barkley Owens, *Cormac McCarthy's Western Novels* (Tucson: University of Arizona Press, 2000), 66.

11. Owens, 68.

12. Ibid., 65.

13. *All the Pretty Horses*, 299.

14. Ibid., 242.

15. Cormac McCarthy, *The Crossing* (New York: Vintage, 1995), 4.

16. Ibid, 127.

Chapter 5. How It All Ends: *The Road* and the End of History

1. Cormac McCarthy, *The Road* (New York: Knopf, 2006), 83.
2. Ibid., 283.
3. Ibid., 21.
4. Susan Sontag, "The Imagination of Disaster," in *Commentary* (October 1965), 44–45.
5. *The Road*, 149–150.
6. Sontag, 45.
7. Ibid.
8. *The Road*, 25.
9. Ibid, 213.
10. Ibid., 3.
11. Ibid., 28.
12. Ibid., 4.
13. Harold Bloom, *The Western Canon* (London: Riverhead Books, 1995), 30.
14. *The Road*, 75.
15. Ibid., 24.
16. Ibid., 194.
17. Ibid., 9.
18. Ibid., 4.
19. Michail Michajlovic Bakhtin and Michael Holquist, "Forms of Time and of the Chronotope in the Novel," The Dialogic Imagination: Four Essays (Austin: Univ. of Texas Press, 2011), 89.
20. Robert Alter, *Pen of Iron: American Prose and the King James Bible* (Princeton, NJ: Princeton University Press, 2010), 1.
21. Ibid., 2.

22. Ibid.
23. Ibid., 4.
24. Ibid., 5.
25. Michael Chabon, *Maps and Legends: Reading and Writing Along the Borderlands* (San Francisco: McSweeney's Books, 2008), 113.
26. *The Road*, 28.
27. Ibid., 27.
28. Ibid., 47.
29. E.D.W. Lynch, "Chipotle Mexican Grill," *Yelping with Cormac*, January 3, 2012, yelpingwithcormac.tumblr.com/search/chipotle+grill.

LITERARY TERMS

allegory—A story that contains a hidden moral or meaning.

archetypical—A recurring theme, setting, image, or character that seems to represent some part of a universal human nature. For example, a hero is an archetypical character, as is a father figure or mother figure. A garden might stand as an archetype of paradise.

bildungsroman—A novel (German: *bildung:* "education" + Roman: "novel") that has to do with a young person growing up, developing, or coming of age.

dichotomy—A contrast or an opposition between two things, such as religion and science, or dark and light.

florid—Extremely complicated or elaborate.

foil—A character or object that is used in a narrative to highlight qualities in a different character; for example, a villain might act as a foil by presenting a challenge to the hero, who displays wisdom in overcoming the situation.

imagery—The use of visual metaphors and figurative language to create meaning or depth.

in media res—Latin phrase that means "into the middle of things"; used to describe a story that begins in the middle of the action, rather than at the beginning of a chronological tale.

irony—When meaning is different from use, or when what comes to pass is not typical or expected; sarcasm and satire are forms of verbal irony.

metaphor—A figure of language identifying two things that are not similar in order to enhance the meaning or significance of something; for example, "The man was a lion, strong and brave" identifies a man with a lion based on the similarity of their qualities.

parable—A short story that teaches a lesson or illustrates a religious principle.

parataxis—Clauses one after another with coordinating conjunctions; clauses might occur in a long list.

redemption—The act of saving someone who is considered lost.

simile—Relating two unlike things using *as* or *like*; for example, "The man was as strong as a lion."

trajectory— The movement of a story. In literature, a narrative or story often moves along a line, from then to now (temporal), or from here to there (spatial). The arc or trajectory of a narrative can sometimes resemble the flight of an arrow: starting here, ending there, and having different levels of tension in between.

Major Works by Cormac McCarthy

Novels

The Orchard Keeper (1965)
Outer Dark (1968)
Child of God (1973)
Suttree (1979)
Blood Meridian, or the Evening Redness in the West (1985)
All the Pretty Horses (1992)
The Crossing (1994)
Cities of the Plain (1998)
No Country for Old Men (2005)
The Road (2006)

Screenplays

The Gardener's Son (1976)
The Sunset Limited (2011)
The Counselor (2013)

Plays

The Stonemason (1995)
The Sunset Limited (2006)

Further Reading

Anderson, Eric Gary, Taylor Hagood, and Daniel Cross Turner, eds. *Undead Souths: The Gothic and Beyond in Southern Literature and Culture*. Baton Rouge: Louisiana State University Press, 2015.

Bloom, Harold. *Cormac McCarthy*. New York: Chelsea House Publications, 2009.

Ciuba, Gary. *Desire, Violence, and Divinity in Modern Southern Fiction: Katherine Anne Porter, Flannery O'Connor, Cormac McCarthy, Walker Percy*. Baton Rouge: Louisiana State University Press, 2011.

Kaplan, E. Ann. *Climate Trauma: Foreseeing the Future in Dystopian Film and Fiction*. New Brunswick, NJ: Rutgers University Press, 2015.

Pagels, Elaine. *The Gnostic Gospels*. New York: Vintage, 1989.

WEBSITES

The Official Website of the Cormac McCarthy Society
www.cormacmccarthy.com
Includes biography, resources, forum, and overviews of McCarthy texts.

Oprah's Exclusive Interview with Cormac McCarthy
www.oprah.com/oprahsbookclub/Oprahs-Exclusive-Inter-view-with-Cormac-McCarthy-Video -
Video of McCarthy's 2007 sit-down with the talk-show host.

INDEX